W9-AMC-408

American Corn

Also by Maria Polushkin Robbins

The Cook's Quotation Book
The Dumpling Cookbook
Blue-Ribbon Pies
Blue-Ribbon Pickles & Preserves
Blue-Ribbon Cookies

American Corn

Maria Polushkin Robbins

ST. MARTIN'S PRESS ♦ NEW YORK

AMERICAN CORN. Copyright © 1989 by Maria Polushkin Robbins. All rights reserved. Printed in the United States of America. No part of this book may be used or reproduced in any manner whatsoever without written permission except in the case of brief quotations embodied in critical articles or reviews. For information, address St. Martin's Press, 175 Fifth Avenue, New York, N.Y. 10010.

Library of Congress Cataloging-in-Publication Data

Robbins, Maria Polushkin.
    American corn / Maria Polushkin Robbins.
      p. cm.
    ISBN 0-312-02861-X
    1. Cookery (Corn) 2. Cookery, American. I. Title.
  TX809.M2P65 1989   88-36474
  641.6′315—dc19   CIP

First Edition

10 9 8 7 6 5 4 3 2 1

To Ken

I am especially grateful to my editor, Barbara Anderson, and for help from my friends, Genie Chipps Henderson, Claudia Jessup, Dava Sobel, Lauren Jarrett, Kate O'Brien, Clare O'Brien, and Maggie Kotuk. I am also grateful to Nick and Toni whose wonderful restaurant always restores the body and refreshes the soul.

Contents

They eat the Indian corn in a great variety of forms . . . .

—Frances Trollope,
  Domestic Manners of the Americans, 1832

INTRODUCTION

People say, ". . . as American as apple pie," but when it comes to food, nothing, not even apple pie, is as purely American as corn. *Zea mays* (to give it its botanical name) is, in fact, the only truly indigenous American grain—all others having been brought here by settlers—and so it is not a little ironic that while the rest of the world knows it as "maize," a Native American word, we Americans call it corn, a generic European term for any sort of grain.

Call it what you will, corn was a staple of human consumption for five thousand years before the first Europeans set foot on this continent. And when they did arrive, it was corn that got them through the first terrible winters when their barley crops failed.

It's said, too, that the Plymouth colonists, lacking dairy cattle, made do with an ersatz milk made from the juices of corn, chestnuts, and hickory nuts. Other early settlers derived a sugar from the stalks of the corn plant, and porridge (variously known as hasty pudding or samp or mush) was in many places a staple.

From the Indians the colonists learned to make several kinds of corn bread, including corn pone, which was baked in an oven; hoecakes, which were literally grilled on a hoe over an open flame; and ashcakes, which, as the name implies, were baked in the ashes of a hearthfire.

In the centuries that followed, corn was so intensively cultivated and hybridized that "corn-fed" has become synonymous with American wholesomeness, and corn has become one of the most important cash crops and sources of human nutrition in the world.

Of course, more corn is eaten by livestock than by humans, partly because corn was once widely (and still, though more rarely) considered fit only for fodder. More generally, though, the reason has to do with the demand, at least among the wealthier peoples of the world, for corn-fed beef, pork, chicken, and the like. Still, in North America we directly consume over four bushels a year for every man, woman, and child; and this in every imaginable form from cornflakes to corn on the cob, from popcorn to corn bread. In view of its popularity, it is good to know that corn is good for us. Combined with beans or a small amount of a dairy product, such as milk or cheese, corn is an excellent source of protein and a good source of dietary fiber. Not only that, but studies now show that corn bran can lower cholesterol as much if not more than oat bran.

Taken all in all, corn is truly one of the most amazingly versatile, delicious, and important foodstuffs known to man. If you doubt it, just try a few of the recipes in this book and see if you don't change your mind.

A Word About Basic Ingredients

Butter. All the butter called for is unsalted or "sweet" butter. You may substitute an equal amount of margarine or vegetable oil if you wish.

Cornmeal. Whether you use yellow or white cornmeal, make sure it is stone-ground. Stone-ground cornmeal retains the nutritious germ and has better flavor than commercially ground cornmeal. Yellow cornmeal has slightly more vitamin A, but otherwise the yellow and white are interchangeable. Try to buy stone-ground cornmeal from a reliable source such as the mill itself or a good health-food store. Store stone-ground cornmeal in the refrigerator. Avoid, if possible, degerminated cornmeal found on supermarket shelves. The difference in flavor and nutritional value between these commercial cornmeals and stone-ground cornmeal is astonishing.

Here are several good mail order sources for stone-ground cornmeal:

Morgan's Mills
RD 2
Box 115
Union, Maine 04862
Telephone: 207-785-4900

Kenyon Cornmeal Company
Usquepaugh, Rhode Island 02892
Telephone: 401-783-4054

For blue cornmeal:

Blue Corn Connection
3825 Academy Parkway South NE
Albuquerque, New Mexico 87109
Telephone: 505-344-9768

Flour. Unless otherwise specified, all flour called for in this book is unbleached all-purpose flour.

Olive oil. Olive oil is often more than just the cooking medium but is an important flavoring agent as well. Try to use the best: extra virgin cold-pressed olive oil. Store in a cool dark place.

Vegetable oil. My favorites are sunflower and safflower oil, but corn oil is good, too.

Corn on the Cob

How to Buy It and
Prepare It
Butters to Enhance It

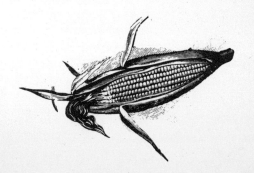

• CORN ON THE COB •

Sweet corn on the cob is one of the great glories of summer. Quickly boiled, anointed with butter, and seasoned with salt is the way most Americans enjoy their corn, most of the time. Next to tomatoes, it is probably America's favorite vegetable.

• HOW TO BUY IT •

Everyone knows that the best way to have the freshest, sweetest corn on the cob is to grow it yourself, and, when it is ripe, set a kettle of water on to boil as you are going out to pick the ears. Actually, corn that fresh is delicious without any cooking at all. If you ever have the chance to try some very freshly picked corn, pull away the husks, strip away the silks, and bite right in. The corn will be juicy and unbelievably sweet. And this is the best way to know, once and for all, how little cooking fresh corn needs.

But what if you can't grow your own corn? Here's what you need to know: As soon as the corn is picked, the natural sugar in the corn begins to turn to starch. This process happens very quickly and only two conditions help to slow it down—keeping the corn cold and moist. So when you buy your corn—ideally from the farmer who grew it, picked it that morning, and kept it cool and shaded until he sold it to you—get it home as quickly as possible and into the refrigerator the minute you walk in the door. When I go shopping in the height of summer, when shopping means driving around from one favorite vegetable stand to another, I set out with a huge ice-cooled picnic cooler in the trunk of my car. The corn I buy goes directly into the cooler and then I can tarry as long as I please without worrying that the delicious corn is turning to tasteless mealy mush.

If you can't buy directly from the farmer who grows the corn, go to a good greengrocer or a supermarket that takes care and pride in its produce. Don't buy any corn that hasn't been kept cool and damp. The ears of corn should look full and plump and the green husks should look fresh and tightly closed around the ear. If possible, check an ear by pulling back the husk and piercing a kernel with a fingernail. If the corn is ripe and fresh, corn "milk" should spurt from the kernel. If the corn is mealy and dry, it has been around too long.

◆ HOW TO HUSK IT ◆

Just before cooking, peel away the green husks and pull away the silk around the kernels.

If you are going to cook the corn in the husks, peel down the husks, but don't remove them, pull away as much of the silk as possible, then wrap the husks back around the ear, twisting them or tying them at the top.

• HOW TO FREEZE CORN ON THE COB •

It is worth it to freeze your own corn when you can get the freshest sweet corn available. Remove the husks and silks. Pack the ears of corn in plastic freezer bags and seal tightly. You don't need to thaw the corn before cooking; simply add 20 minutes to the cooking time. You can keep corn frozen for six months to a year.

• HOW TO COOK CORN ON THE COB •

Boiling. Everybody, it seems, has his own perfect method for boiling corn, and most of them are fine as long as they don't involve cooking the corn for a prolonged length of time. I consider my way both foolproof and easy. Fill a very large pot about two-thirds full of water. Do not add salt. Do not add sugar. The salt will make the corn tough. The sugar isn't necessary. When the water comes to a boil, drop the corn into the water and watch it. As soon as it returns to a boil, remove from heat and let stand for 5 minutes. At this point the corn can rest in the hot water for as long as 20 minutes.

Steaming. Stand the husked ears upright, stalk end down, in a tall pot. Or place the shucked corn on a rack inside a steamer. Add water to a depth of about 2 inches. Bring to a boil, cover the pot, and steam the corn 10 minutes.

Oven Roasting. Preheat oven to 400° F. Peel down the husks, but don't remove them. Pull away as much of the silk as possible, then wrap the husks back around the ear, twisting them or tying them at the top. Soak the corn in cold water for 10 minutes (this keeps them from drying out while roasting). Place corn on rack in oven and bake for 20 minutes.

Oven roasting is a particularly good way to cook frozen ears of corn. Do not defrost, but brush corn with melted butter and wrap each ear in aluminum foil, twisting the foil tightly shut at both ends. Bake for 45 to 50 minutes.

Grilling. When you are barbecuing, it is easy to include corn among the items that get cooked over the hot coals. Cooked this way, the corn gets a delicious smoky flavor.

If you are eating outdoors and messiness is not a consideration, you can cook whole ears of corn over hot coals with no preliminary preparation. Place the corn on the grill and turn often with long-handled tongs, for 15 to 20 minutes. Tear away the blistered husks and silks as soon as corn is cool enough to handle (everyone seems to have his or her own level of tolerance).

For a neater result, peel down the husks, but don't remove them. Pull away as much of the silk as possible, then wrap the husks back around the ear, twisting them or tying them at the top. Soak the corn in cold water for 10 minutes (this keeps them from drying out while grilling). Cook over hot coals for 15 to 20 minutes, turning them often with long-handled tongs.

Though the number of rows on an ear of corn may vary from variety to variety, there are always an even number of rows.

◆ CHILI BUTTER ◆

½ cup butter or margarine, softened to
   room temperature

1 teaspoon chili powder
¼ teaspoon pepper

In a small bowl combine butter or margarine and the seasonings. Mash and beat with a wooden spoon until well blended.

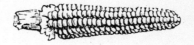

I planted corn and I have here not only a crop of corn but of happiness and hope. My tilled fields have miraculously sprung up to friends.

—*David Grayson,*
Adventures in Contentment

◆ CHIVE OR SCALLION BUTTER ◆

½ cup butter or margarine, softened to
   room temperature

2 teaspoons chopped chives or scallions
1 teaspoon lemon juice

In a small bowl combine butter or margarine and the seasonings. Mash and beat with a wooden spoon until well blended.

◆ DILL BUTTER ◆

½ cup butter or margarine, softened to
   room temperature

1 teaspoon fresh chopped dill

In a small bowl combine butter or margarine and the seasonings. Mash and beat with a wooden spoon until well blended.

• CAJUN BUTTER •

*½ cup butter or margarine, softened to
  room temperature*
1½ teaspoons paprika
1 teaspoon dried thyme

1 teaspoon dried oregano
¼ teaspoon cayenne
¼ teaspoon freshly ground black pepper
Several dashes Tabasco

In a small bowl combine butter or margarine and the seasonings. Mash and beat
with a wooden spoon until well blended.

• PESTO BUTTER •

*½ cup butter or margarine, softened to
  room temperature*
¼ cup fresh basil leaves, finely shredded

1 garlic clove, finely minced
*2 tablespoons freshly grated Parmesan
  cheese*

In a small bowl combine butter or margarine and the seasonings. Mash and beat
with a wooden spoon until well blended.

◆ LEMON-PEPPER BUTTER ◆

½ cup butter or margarine
¼ cup fresh lemon juice

1 teaspoon salt
Freshly ground black pepper to taste

Melt the butter or margarine in a large skillet. Remove from heat, stir in lemon juice, salt, and freshly ground black pepper. Place a couple of ears of hot cooked corn in the skillet and roll around. Remove the ears to a large heated platter. Continue until all the ears are buttered.

◆ CUMIN BUTTER ◆

½ cup butter or margarine, softened to
    room temperature
1 tablespoon ground cumin

1 teaspoon salt
¼ teaspoon cayenne
1 lime, cut into wedges

Melt the butter or margarine in a large skillet. Remove from heat, stir in cumin, salt, and cayenne. Place a couple of ears of hot cooked corn in the skillet and roll around. Remove the ears to a large heated platter. Continue until all the ears are buttered. Serve with lime wedges.

◆ CHINESE HERB BUTTER ◆

½ cup butter or margarine
1 tablespoon finely chopped fresh ginger

½ teaspoon Szechuan peppercorns
1 teaspoon oyster sauce

Melt the butter or margarine in a large skillet. Add the ginger and peppercorns. Cook over medium heat, stirring, for 1 minute. Remove from heat and stir in the oyster sauce. Place a couple of ears of hot cooked corn in the skillet and roll around. Remove the ears to a large heated platter. Continue until all the ears are buttered.

They delight much to feed on Roasting-ears; that is, the Indian corn, gathered green and milky, before it is grown to its full bigness, and roasted before the fire, in the Ear. . . . And this indeed is a very sweet and pleasing food.

*—William Byrd, writing about the
Indians in Virginia, 1737*

Corn off the Cob

Appetizers

Salads

Side Dishes

◆ FRESH CORN KERNELS OFF THE COB ◆

When fresh corn first comes into season it is hard to see why you should bother having it any other way than on the cob. But as summer progresses and we have sated our first hunger for fresh corn, the myriad dishes that feature fresh corn kernels cut or scraped off the cob hold great appeal. Corn is the most companionable of vegetables and it mingles easily and well with so many other flavors and textures that it is worth the slight trouble of removing the kernels from the cobs to make succotash, chowder, corn pudding, a mixed summer salad, pasta with fresh corn, or any of a number of delicious dishes.

There are two ways of cutting corn from the cob: the "cut" method results in whole kernels. The "scrape" or "shave" method extracts the inner flesh of the corn kernels along with the "milk." The cut kernels are good to use in salads and other dishes where the texture of the whole kernel is important. Scraped corn is good for chowders, corn cakes, and puddings.

To cut corn kernels away from the cob, stand the shucked corncob on end in a soup bowl or pie plate and slice down with a small sharp knife, away from yourself, cutting three or four rows at a time.

To "scrape" or "shave" corn kernels, stand the shucked corncob on end in a soup bowl or pie plate and use a small sharp knife to cut down the center of each row, cutting only about one-half the depth of the kernels. Use the back of the knife to scrape out the rest of the pulp and milk.

◆ FROZEN CORN KERNELS ◆

To freeze your own corn kernels, cut kernels away from the cob as described above. Store in plastic freezer bags or boxes in one- to two-cup portions. Seal tightly and freeze. These corn kernels can be used in any recipe without thawing.

Keep in mind that there are excellent varieties of commercially frozen corn that can be used in place of freshly cut corn kernels when corn is not in season.

From the United States every year a kind friend sent a little packet of sweet-corn seed grown and gathered by his mother. It was a great treat for us. At that time there was no table corn in France. The French grew corn for animals—in the Bugey, for the chickens. When it was known that we were growing it and eating it, they considered us savages. No one was seduced by the young ears we gave them to taste.

—*Alice B. Toklas,* The Alice B. Toklas Cookbook

◆ AMERICAN RATATOUILLE ◆

1 large onion, chopped fine
2 cloves garlic, minced
3 to 4 tablespoons olive oil
1 jalapeño pepper, seeded and sliced into
    thin strips (optional)
3 to 4 large ripe tomatoes, peeled, seeded,
    and chopped
1 cup fresh or frozen lima beans
2 small zucchini, cut into ½-inch chunks

2 cups fresh pumpkin, cut into ¾-inch
    chunks
2 cups fresh corn kernels (about 4 ears of
    corn)
¼ cup thinly sliced basil leaves
¼ cup finely chopped parsley
Salt to taste
Freshly ground black pepper to taste

In a large sauté pan, cook onions and garlic in olive oil until softened, about 10 minutes. Add the jalapeño pepper, tomatoes, lima beans, zucchini, and pumpkin. Cook over medium heat, stirring frequently, until vegetables are almost done, about 15 to 20 minutes. Add corn kernels, basil, parsley, salt, and pepper and cook 5 minutes longer. Serve hot or at room temperature.

Yield: 6 servings

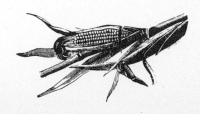

◆ GRILLED OYSTERS WITH CORN VINAIGRETTE ◆

These make ideal hors d'oeuvres for informal summer get-togethers, especially when you've got the grill going anyway.

¾ cup olive oil
¼ cup balsamic vinegar
¼ cup dry red wine
6 basil leaves, finely shredded
3 shallots, finely minced

2 cups fresh corn kernels (about 4 ears of corn)
Salt to taste
Freshly ground black pepper to taste
3 dozen oysters in their shells

In a bowl, whisk together the olive oil, balsamic vinegar, and red wine. Stir in basil, shallots, and corn kernels, and salt and freshly ground black pepper. Cover and let stand for at least an hour (can be done several hours ahead).

Scrub the oysters. Grill them over hot coals until oysters pop open. Remove with tongs to a platter and discard top shell. Garnish each oyster with approximately 1 tablespoon of the corn vinaigrette. Serve warm or at room temperature.

Yield: 8–12 appetizer portions

◆ CORN OYSTERS ◆

Serve these to guests as an hors d'oeuvre or make a meal of them for brunch or lunch.

4 cups fresh corn kernels (about 8 ears of
   corn)
4 egg yolks
1 teaspoon sugar
½ teaspoon salt

Freshly ground black pepper to taste
½ cup all-purpose flour
3 egg whites
4 to 6 tablespoons vegetable oil for frying

Place 3½ cups corn kernels in the bowl of a blender or food processor and process for a few seconds until corn kernels are broken up to a grated texture. Remove creamed corn kernels to a large mixing bowl and add the remaining ½ cup corn kernels, egg yolks, sugar, salt, and black pepper. Mix well, then stir in flour.

Beat egg whites until they form stiff peaks, then fold gently into the corn kernel mixture.

Heat enough oil to cover the bottom of a frying pan. Drop the batter by tablespoonfuls into the hot oil. Cook until golden brown on both sides. Keep fritters warm in a 250° F. oven until ready to serve. Serve with your favorite chutney, salsa, or jalapeño jelly.

Yield: 25–30 fritters

• CORN PIE •

Serve this American-style quiche as a light lunch or an appetizer.

1 unbaked 9-inch pie shell
3 ears sweet corn
4 eggs
½ cup grated mild cheese (Monterey Jack
   or Muenster)
½ cup heavy cream
½ cup sour cream

1 small onion, chopped very fine or grated
1 fresh or canned green chili pepper,
   chopped fine (optional)
1 teaspoon salt, or to taste
Freshly ground black pepper to taste
Dash of Tabasco

Preheat oven to 450° F. Partially bake the pie crust: Butter a round of aluminum foil and place inside the pie crust—fill with rice or beans and bake at 450° F. for 5 to 7 minutes. Remove aluminum foil and rice or beans.

Scrape the corn by standing the shucked corncob on end in a soup bowl or pie plate and use a small sharp knife to cut down the center of each row, cutting only about one-half the depth of the kernels. Use the back of the knife to scrape out the rest of the pulp and milk. You should have about 1½ cups of corn kernels.

Beat the eggs in a large bowl, add the grated cheese, heavy cream, sour cream, corn kernels, onion, and green chili pepper, then stir. Add the salt, black pepper, and Tabasco. Taste and adjust seasoning.

Pour into pie shell. Bake for 10 minutes at 450° F., then lower temperature to 350° F. and bake for another 20 to 25 minutes, until top is golden brown and somewhat firm. Let cool about 15 to 20 minutes before serving or cool completely and serve at room temperature.

Yield: 6–8 servings

• SPICY CORN SALAD •

2 cups cooked corn kernels
1 green bell pepper, roasted, peeled,
  seeded, and chopped
1 red bell pepper, roasted, peeled, seeded,
  and chopped
1 fresh or canned jalapeño pepper,
  seeded, deveined, and chopped
  (optional)

2 ribs celery, finely diced
1 small red onion, finely diced
½ cup olive oil
¼ cup cider vinegar
¼ cup finely chopped parsley
1 tablespoon finely chopped coriander
Salt to taste
Freshly ground black pepper to taste

Combine all the ingredients in a salad bowl and mix well.

Yield: 4–6 normal servings, but in my house there is only enough for one serving, mine!

Corn in Mexico at the time of Cortez was so plentiful that it was often planted by the sides of the roads as a kind of free sustenance for the hungry traveler. Hunger was virtually unknown to the Aztecs of that time, thanks to maize.

⋆ CLAUDIA'S SOUTHWESTERN CORN SALAD ⋆

3 cups cooked corn kernels★
1 medium red onion, cut lengthwise in
   thin slices, then cut the slices in half
1 ripe avocado, cut in small cubes and
   sprinkled with lemon juice
1–2 jalapeño peppers, minced (or use
   canned green chilies to make the dish
   less hot)

½ cup finely minced cilantro leaves
⅓ cup olive oil
2 tablespoons balsamic vinegar (or 1
   tablespoon red wine vinegar)
Salt to taste
Black pepper to taste

In a salad bowl, mix together the corn kernels, onion, avocado, and jalapeños. Toss in cilantro, then add oil, vinegar, salt, and pepper. Mix well and let stand several hours before serving. This salad keeps well refrigerated for several days.

Yield: 8–10 servings

The number of kernels found on an ear of corn will vary with the size of the corncob. I have gotten a yield of anywhere from ¼ cup to ¾ cup from one corncob. On the average I figure that one ear of corn yields ½ cup corn kernels.

★This salad is delicious using canned or frozen corn kernels.

Before Columbus came home from the Americas, nobody in Europe had ever seen or tasted:

1. *turkey or guinea fowl or turtle meat*
2. *peanuts, cashew nuts, black walnuts, Brazil nuts, or butternuts*
3. *pineapple or papaya*
4. *potatoes or sweet potatoes*
5. *tomatoes*
6. *kidney beans, lima beans, navy beans, or string beans*
7. *squashes or pumpkins*
8. *avocados*
9. *allspice*
10. *peppers, not the spice but the fruit, Capsicums: bell peppers, chili peppers, cayenne peppers, etc.*

—*list based on information found in* The Food Book, *by James Trager*

◆ BLACK BEAN AND CORN SALAD ◆

I make this salad all year round—in the summer with leftover kernels from corn on the cob, in the winter with frozen corn kernels. It alternates with tuna fish salad as a lunch staple in my house. I have also found versions of it in fancy food stores selling for upward of $6.00 a pound!

4 cups cooked black beans (if canned, rinse well under cold running water)
2 cups cooked corn kernels
2 large ripe tomatoes, roughly chopped (only in season)
1 large red bell pepper, seeded and chopped into small pieces
2 stalks celery, chopped
1 small red onion, chopped fine
or

5 scallions, chopped fine
½ cup finely chopped parsley
¼ cup finely chopped fresh coriander
1 garlic clove
1 teaspoon salt
1 teaspoon cumin seeds
½ cup olive oil
Juice of ½ lime
Tabasco to taste
Freshly ground black pepper to taste

In a large bowl, combine the beans, corn kernels, tomatoes, red bell pepper, celery, onion or scallions, parsley, and coriander. With a mortar and pestle, crush the garlic clove with the salt and cumin seeds to make a paste. Whisk in the olive oil and lime juice. Add Tabasco. Pour the dressing over the bean salad and mix well. Taste for seasoning and add freshly ground black pepper.

Yield: 6–8 servings

Variations: You can make changes to suit your taste. Leave out coriander and cumin if you don't like them. Substitute lemon juice or balsamic vinegar for the lime juice. When there are no ripe tomatoes, substitute a couple of sun-dried tomatoes. If you have a ripe avocado, chop it up and toss it in. If you like spicy food, toss in some chopped green chilies or jalapeño pepper.

> *Corn by the common usage is eaten from the cob, but the exhibition is not interesting.*
>
> —Gentle Manners, A Guide to Good Morals
> *Shaker, Anonymous*

• SPICY ITALIAN CORN SALAD •

This salad is so good that it is worth making from scratch; in other words, cook the corn just for the salad. Don't wait for leftovers.

3 large ripe tomatoes
3 cups cooked corn kernels
4 scallions, finely chopped, green part
* included*
1 small fresh green chili or jalapeño
* pepper, seeded and finely minced*

2 or 3 large basil leaves, finely shredded
¼ cup olive oil
2 tablespoons balsamic vinegar
½ teaspoon Dijon mustard
½ teaspoon salt
Freshly ground black pepper to taste

Dice the tomatoes and place in a salad bowl. (If you're feeling fancy you can peel them and seed them, but I usually don't bother.) Add the corn kernels, scallions, chili or jalapeño pepper, and basil. In a small bowl combine the olive oil, vinegar, mustard, salt, and pepper. Mix well with a fork. Toss the vegetables with the olive oil dressing and serve.

Yield: 6 servings

◆ WILD RICE AND CORN SALAD ◆

4 cups water
1 teaspoon salt
2/3 cup wild rice
2 ripe tomatoes
3 scallions
1 cup cooked corn kernels

1/4 cup olive oil
2 tablespoons balsamic vinegar
Salt to taste
Freshly ground black pepper to taste
1/4 cup slivered almonds, toasted
Washed lettuce greens

Bring the water and salt to a boil in a large saucepan. Add the wild rice, reduce heat, and simmer, partly covered, until tender, about 40 minutes. Drain and rinse rice under cold water.

Peel, seed, and dice the tomatoes. Chop scallions, including the green tops. In a bowl, combine the wild rice, tomatoes, scallions, and corn kernels.

In a small bowl, whisk together the olive oil, balsamic vinegar, and salt and pepper. Pour over wild rice–corn mixture and toss. Adjust seasoning to taste. Let stand, covered, at room temperature until ready to serve. (You can prepare this several hours ahead.) Add toasted, slivered almonds, toss, and serve on lettuce greens.

Yield: 4 servings

• FRIED CORN •

The great taste of corn on the cob without the messy work of eating it that way. Make this when you feel self-indulgent or for a fancy meal.

8 to 12 ears of corn
1 stick butter

1 teaspoon salt
Freshly ground black pepper to taste

Husk the corn and cut the kernels away from the cobs. Melt the butter in a large skillet or sauté pan over medium heat until it sizzles. Add the corn kernels and sauté for 4 to 5 minutes, shaking the pan and stirring often so that the corn does not stick. Remove from heat and season with salt and pepper.

Yield: 6–8 servings

Variations:
1. Add any fresh herb you like, such as basil, dill, thyme, or parsley.
2. Add ½ cup heavy cream and cook over high heat to thicken.
3. Add 4 or 5 finely sliced scallions.
4. Add 1 red bell pepper, cored, seeded, and finely chopped.

• BAKED CORN •

Make this when you have had your fill of corn on the cob, and all the other ways of eating fresh corn kernels. The long baking time makes for a crusty, crispy, and very comforting dish of corn.

1 stick butter
8–10 ears of corn
1 tablespoon sugar

1 teaspoon salt
Freshly ground black pepper to taste

Preheat oven to 375°F. Spread half the butter all over the inside of a 9-inch Pyrex pie plate. Scrape the corn by standing the shucked corncob on end in a soup bowl or pie plate and using a small sharp knife to cut down the center of each row, cutting only about one-half the depth of the kernels. Use the back of the knife to scrape out the rest of the pulp and milk. In a bowl combine the corn kernels, sugar, salt, and pepper and mix well. Place corn mixture in pie plate and dot with remaining butter. Bake 45 minutes or until the top is golden brown and very crisp.

Yield: 4–6 servings

◆ SWEET CORN WITH PEPPERS ◆

4 green, red, or yellow bell peppers in any
  combination
2 tablespoons olive oil
1 tablespoon butter
2 large cloves garlic, minced

2 cups freshly cut corn kernels (about 4
  ears of corn)
⅔ cup finely chopped scallions
Salt to taste
Freshly ground black pepper to taste

Remove the veins and seeds from the peppers and cut them into very thin strips.

Heat the oil and butter in a skillet or sauté pan over medium heat until they sizzle, then add the peppers and garlic. Cook, stirring and shaking, for about 5 minutes. Add corn kernels, scallions, and salt and pepper to taste. Cook for another 5 minutes, stirring often. Peppers should retain some of their crunch.

Serve as a vegetable side dish or serve over your favorite pasta with freshly grated Parmesan cheese.

Yield: 6 servings

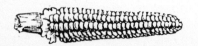

• MARIA'S FRIED CORN •

2 large potatoes (russet or Idaho)
4 tablespoons sunflower oil
2 onions
6 ears leftover cooked corn on the cob

1 chipotle pepper*
⅓ cup chopped parsley
Salt to taste
Freshly ground black pepper to taste

Scrub and dice the potatoes. Heat the oil in a heavy black cast-iron skillet and sauté the potatoes at rather high heat. Flip them over and around from time to time with a spatula, scraping the bottom of the skillet so the spuds don't stick. Dice the onion and add it to the potatoes after they have started to brown slightly, 10 or 15 minutes. Stir and continue to cook. Slice the kernels off the corn and add to the potato-onion mixture. Stir and continue cooking ten minutes more. Chop the chipotle pepper, add to the vegetables, and cook, stirring, for 5 more minutes. Add parsley, salt, and freshly ground black pepper. Taste for seasoning, adjust, and serve.

Serve with a garlicky green salad and some crusty bread.

Yield: 4 servings

---

*Chipotle peppers are smoked jalapeño peppers in a spicy marinade. They come canned and, once removed to a plastic or glass container, last indefinitely in the refrigerator. I cannot live without them but they are hard to find. Check out Latin-American and Mexican-American markets and any store that carries ingredients from the American Southwest. If you cannot find them substitute red hot pepper flakes to taste.

◆ CORN PUDDING ◆

8 ears of sweet corn (about 4 cups of corn kernels)
3 eggs
1 pint heavy cream
3 tablespoons melted butter

2 teaspoons sugar
1 teaspoon salt or to taste
Freshly ground black pepper to taste
A pinch of cayenne
A few drops of Tabasco sauce

Preheat oven to 350° F.

Scrape the corn by standing the shucked corncob on end in a soup bowl or pie plate and using a small sharp knife to cut down the center of each row, cutting only about one-half the depth of the kernels. Use the back of the knife to scrape out the rest of the pulp and milk.

Beat the eggs in a large bowl and add the cream, melted butter, sugar, and all seasonings. Pour into a buttered 1½-quart baking dish. Set the baking dish into a pan of hot water and place on middle rack in oven. Bake 35–40 minutes. The pudding is done when a sharp knife inserted in center comes out clean.

Yield: 6–8 servings

"Green corn," in old recipes and cookbooks, refers to fresh corn on the cob.

◆ YELLOW VELVET ◆

The colorful name comes from the Shakers; the delicate, delicious flavor comes from the perfect combination of sweet corn and yellow summer squash. For the best flavor, buy the smallest squashes you can find and use the freshest corn.

*2 pounds small yellow summer squash
(the smaller the better)
5 ears fresh corn
4 tablespoons butter*

*⅓ cup heavy cream
Salt to taste
Freshly ground black pepper to taste*

Wash and trim the squash and cut into tiny cubes.

Cut the corn kernels from the cobs, keeping your knife perpendicular so that only the tips of the kernels are removed. Then scrape the cobs with the back of the knife to get all the milk and the remaining kernel hearts.

Melt the butter in a skillet or sauté pan over medium heat until it sizzles, then sauté the squash, stirring frequently, for about 5 minutes. Stir the corn kernels into the squash and cook, stirring, for 1 minute more. Add the cream and cook, stirring, for about 3 minutes, to heat through. Add salt and pepper, stir, and serve immediately.

Yield: 4–6 servings

Note: You can substitute evaporated milk for the heavy cream.

• SIMPLE SUCCOTASH •

This simple, delicious mélange is good during the summer or winter. Scrumptious when made with fresh beans and corn, it's really good using the frozen substitutes.

3 cups water
1½ cups fresh lima beans, shelled
    or
1 package frozen baby lima beans
4 tablespoons butter
2 cups fresh, cooked, or frozen corn
   kernels (about 4 ears of corn)

2 tablespoons heavy cream or crème
   fraîche
Salt to taste
Freshly ground black pepper to taste

Bring the water to a boil and add the fresh or frozen beans. Cook for 5 to 10 minutes until beans are tender. Drain. Melt the butter in a skillet and stir in the corn, beans, and heavy cream or crème fraîche. Cook, stirring, for about 5 minutes. Season to taste with salt and pepper.

Yield: 4 servings

Succotash, originally made of corn and kidney beans (today we use lima beans) and perhaps dog meat, all cooked in bear grease, was another Indian dish the Pilgrims adopted. The Narragansett called it misickquatash.

—*James Trager*, The Food Book

Variation: For a fat-free version, substitute ½ cup very rich homemade chicken stock for the butter and cream. Cook over high heat to quickly reduce the stock. Sprinkle with a couple of teaspoons freshly grated Parmesan cheese.

Succotach is the great dish in Plymouth at every celebration of Forefather's Day, December 22. Tradition says it has been made in that town ever since the Pilgrims raised their first corn and beans, and it is supposed they learned to make it from the Indians.

—*Mary J. Lincoln,* Mrs. Lincoln's Boston Cook Book, *1883*

◆ NATURE CONSERVANCY'S CORN ◆

This recipe comes from my friend and neighbor Lauren Jarrett, who makes it every summer in huge vats to feed hundreds of people who turn up for a dinner in support of the Nature Conservancy. "This is a vegetable mix that is pure, pure summer," says Lauren, "equally tasty with barbecued steak, lamb, chicken, or fish, with boiled lobster or a simple tomato vinaigrette. Freeze it and take it camping, or pull it out in coldest February for a needed reminder that spring and summer will come again."

Corn	*Olive oil*
Zucchini	*Bread crumbs, Italian style*
Shallots	*Parmesan cheese, freshly grated*
Scallions	*Salt to taste*
Butter	*Freshly ground black pepper to taste*

Cut the kernels from the cobs of as much corn as you can deal with at one time. The corn should be as fresh as possible. Cut the zucchini into small triangular pieces by cutting lengthwise wedges, then slicing across (the zucchini should make up about ⅓ the volume of the corn).

Mince some shallots. Chop some scallions.

Sauté the shallots in a good bit of half butter and half olive oil. Add the zucchini and cook for 1 minute, stirring. Add the corn, scallions, some Italian-style bread crumbs, some Parmesan cheese, and salt and pepper. Toss it all around until it is creamy and cooked, about 2 minutes.

Yield: 3–350 servings, depending . . .

Variations:

1. You can substitute yellow squash and chopped yellow pepper for the zucchini for an all-yellow mix, or vary the herbs to include basil and parsley.

2. To freeze for camping or winter, mix all the vegetables except shallots. Pack flat in ziplock bags and press out the air. Cook right from the freezer in butter, olive oil, and shallots. Then add the Parmesan cheese and bread crumbs and adjust the seasonings.

After spreading rapidly through Africa, corn actually lost popularity because it was thought to cause pellagra. There is, of course, no causal connection, but corn does lack some vitamins, and thus, nutritious as it is, can cause some problems if relied on exclusively. Early American cultures that supplemented their corn diet with tomatoes, beans, and capsicum (peppers), never suffered from pellagra.

• CLAUDIA'S NEW MEXICAN CORN •

This is a great side dish with chicken or fish, but I've been known to eat it for lunch with some bread or spoon it over scrambled eggs.

1 medium onion, chopped
1 tablespoon olive oil
2 cups tomato puree
2–3 tablespoons red chile powder* (mild, medium, or red hot)

2 tablespoons butter
Salt to taste
Freshly ground black pepper to taste
3 cups fresh, frozen, or canned corn kernels (about 6 ears of corn)

Preheat oven to 350° F.

Sauté onion in olive oil until it starts to turn a golden color (about 15 minutes). Stir in the remaining ingredients and pour into a buttered 2-quart casserole. Bake at 350° F. for 1 hour.

Yield: 6 servings

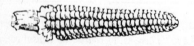

*½ cup diced green chile may be substituted for the red chile powder.

◆ CORN AND OKRA SAUTÉ ◆

1 large onion, finely chopped
1 green bell pepper, seeded and finely chopped
1 fresh jalapeño pepper, seeded and finely chopped
3 tablespoons vegetable oil
3 large ripe tomatoes, peeled, seeded, and finely chopped

½ pound fresh okra, trimmed and cut into ½-inch slices
3 cloves garlic, finely minced
2 cups fresh corn kernels (about 4 ears of corn)
½ teaspoon salt, or to taste
Freshly ground black pepper to taste
¼ teaspoon cayenne, or to taste

Sauté the onion and peppers in the vegetable oil in a large, heavy skillet until they are softened. Add the tomatoes, okra, and garlic, cover, and cook over low heat for about 15 minutes, or until okra is tender. Add the corn kernels, salt, pepper, and cayenne and cook five minutes longer, stirring frequently.

Serve with any grilled fish, shrimp, or chicken or with freshly baked corn bread for a vegetarian lunch.

Yield: 2 main-dish servings or 4 side-dish servings

Note: Like most of the dishes in this book, this one is best made in the summer using fresh ingredients, but this dish works very well in the winter, too. Substitute a 14-ounce can of Italian tomatoes, drained and chopped, for the fresh tomatoes. Substitute frozen okra and frozen corn kernels for the fresh.

Corn in the Pot

Soups and Chowders

• CORN POTATO VICHYSSOISE •

Corn and potatoes make a great combo in this famous cold soup.

4 tablespoons butter
4 medium leeks, white parts only, cut into thin slices
1 medium onion, finely chopped
4 cups chicken stock
4 large russet potatoes, peeled and cut into ½-inch cubes

2 cups fresh corn kernels, (about 4 ears of corn)
2 cups evaporated milk or half-and-half
Salt to taste
White pepper to taste
2 tablespoons finely chopped chives

In a large saucepan, melt the butter and add the leeks and onion. Sauté until soft, about 5 minutes. Add the chicken stock and potatoes and simmer until the potatoes are tender, about 20 minutes. Add the corn kernels and simmer for 10 minutes longer. Remove from heat and puree the soup in small batches in a food processor or blender. Place soup in tureen or large bowl. Stir in the evaporated milk or half-and-half. Taste for seasoning and add salt and white pepper. Refrigerate the soup for several hours until completely chilled. Taste for seasonings and adjust if necessary. Garnish with chives before serving.

Yield: 6 servings

• CORN CHOWDER •

The evaporated milk imparts the rich texture of cream without all the fat. You may substitute regular milk, half-and-half, or heavy cream for some or all of the evaporated milk.

4 slices bacon
1 medium onion, finely chopped
3 celery stalks, finely chopped
5 cups chicken stock
2 large russet potatoes, peeled and cut
   into ½-inch cubes
1 bay leaf
½ teaspoon thyme

3 cups fresh corn kernels (about 6 ears of
   corn)
2 cups evaporated milk
Salt to taste
Freshly ground black pepper to taste
Tabasco to taste
1 tablespoon finely chopped fresh dill

Cook the bacon until crisp. Drain on paper towels and reserve. Take 2 tablespoons of rendered bacon fat and put it in the bottom of a large pot. Sauté onion and celery in the bacon fat until just softened, about 10 minutes. Add the chicken stock, potatoes, bay leaf, and thyme. Bring to a boil, lower heat to a simmer, and cook over low heat until potatoes are soft, about 30 minutes. Use a potato masher to press down and mash some of the potatoes into the soup. Add corn and cook 5 minutes longer. Add evaporated milk and cook over low heat to just heat through. Do not boil. Taste for seasoning and add salt, black pepper, and Tabasco. Garnish with dill.

  Yield: 6 servings

◆ CORN AND SCALLOP CHOWDER ◆

2 tablespoons butter
2 leeks, sliced into thin rounds
4 ears fresh corn
½ cup heavy cream
2 cups fish stock or clam juice*
½ cup dry white wine

Salt to taste
Freshly ground white pepper to taste
Dash of Tabasco
1 pound bay scallops (or sea scallops, quartered)
Finely chopped parsley for garnish

Melt the butter in a heavy saucepan. Sauté the leeks in the butter until wilted but not brown. Remove from heat. Cut corn kernels away from cobs and place them in the bowl of a food processor or blender. Add the sautéed leeks and the heavy cream. Whirl for a few seconds until mixture is smooth. Return mixture to the saucepan and add stock, wine, salt, pepper, and Tabasco. Bring to the boil, reduce heat, and simmer, uncovered, for 5 minutes. Add the scallops and simmer for just 3 minutes more. Remove from heat and serve immediately garnished with parsley.

Yield: 4–6 servings

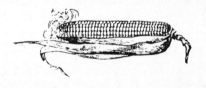

*Or 1 Knorr instant fish flavor bouillon cube dissolved in 2 cups of water.

◆ CORNY FISH CHOWDER ◆

4 slices bacon
1 large onion, finely chopped
2 medium potatoes (russet or Idaho),
    peeled and diced into 1/4-inch pieces
1 1/2 cups water
3 cups milk
1 cup heavy cream
3 cups fresh corn kernels (about 6 ears of
    corn)

1 pound white fish fillet such as haddock,
    halibut, or monkfish, cut into bite-size
    pieces
Salt to taste
Freshly ground black pepper to taste
2 tablespoons finely minced fresh chives

Cook the bacon in a heavy saucepan until crisp and brown. When it is done, remove and drain on paper towels and reserve. Add the onion to the bacon fat and sauté for about 5 minutes, until it turns soft and translucent. Add the diced potatoes, stir well to coat the potatoes, and add the water. Cook over moderate heat for 15 minutes, until the potatoes are almost soft. Add the milk and cream and cook over very low heat until mixture is hot—but do not let it boil. Add the corn kernels and fish. Cook for about 10 minutes over very low heat, never letting the soup come to a boil. Season with salt and pepper. Crumble the reserved bacon and garnish each soup serving with crumbled bacon and minced chives.

Yield: 6 servings

◆ CHICKEN CORN SOUP WITH NOODLES ◆

This Pennsylvania Dutch soup proves that if chicken soup is good for you, then chicken soup with corn is even better. With some good bread and a salad, a bowl of this soup makes a meal.

1 large chicken (about 5 pounds), cut into pieces
4 quarts water
1 medium onion, quartered
2 celery stalks, including leaves, cut into 1-inch pieces
1 carrot, cut into 1-inch pieces

1 tablespoon salt
6 ounces egg noodles
3 cups fresh corn kernels (about 6 ears of corn)
Freshly ground black pepper to taste
¼ cup chopped parsley

Remove the skin and as much visible fat from the chicken as possible. Place the chicken pieces, water, onion, celery, carrot, and salt in a pot and bring to a boil. Lower the heat to a simmer and cook until chicken is tender, 1½ to 2 hours. Remove the chicken from the soup and let cool. Take meat from the bones and discard bones. Shred the chicken into bite-size pieces. Skim as much fat as possible from the stock and return the chicken to the soup. Bring to a boil and add the noodles. Cook about 5 minutes, add corn, and cook 3 to 4 minutes longer, until noodles are just tender. Add salt and pepper to taste and garnish with parsley.

Yield: 6–8 servings

• CORNCOB SOUP •

12 ears of fresh corn
1 onion, peeled and quartered
3 carrots, roughly chopped
4 large celery stalks, roughly chopped
3 cloves garlic, smashed but unpeeled
2 bay leaves
½ bunch parsley, with stalks
3 quarts water
2 tablespoons olive oil
1 onion, chopped
4 large shallots, chopped
2 small zucchini, cut into small dice
1 large red bell pepper, seeded and finely chopped
3 large ripe tomatoes, peeled, seeded, and chopped
1 large garlic clove, minced
1 teaspoon salt
2 tablespoons vegetable oil
2 tablespoons all-purpose flour
6 scallions, thinly sliced, green part included
Freshly ground black pepper to taste

Scrape the corn kernels from 10 corncobs by cutting halfway through the corn kernels all the way down the cob, then, holding the cob over a soup bowl, scrape the

---

Laura had only a corncob wrapped in a handkerchief, but it was a good doll. It was named Susan. It wasn't Susan's fault that she was only a corncob.

—*Laura Ingalls Wilder*, Little House in the Big Woods

---

cob with the dull side of the knife to squeeze out all the "milk." Reserve the kernels and the corn milk. Break the scraped cobs and the remaining 2 whole corncobs in half.

In a large pot, combine the corncobs, quartered onion, carrots, celery, 3 cloves garlic, bay leaves, and parsley. Cover with 3 quarts of water and bring to a boil over high heat and skim off any foam that rises to the surface. Reduce the heat to low and simmer for 2 hours. Remove from heat and strain the stock, discarding corncobs and vegetables. Reserve the stock.

Heat 2 tablespoons of oil in the soup pot, add the chopped onion and shallots, and sauté over medium heat for about 5 minutes, until onions have softened and become translucent. Add zucchini and red bell pepper. Cook, stirring, for about 3 minutes, until vegetables have softened. Add the stock, tomatoes, one clove garlic, and salt. Bring to a boil, lower heat to a simmer, and cook for 30 to 45 minutes.

In another large saucepan or flameproof casserole, blend the oil and flour. Cook over moderate heat, stirring, until golden, about 2 minutes. Add the stock, garlic, and tomatoes. Simmer over moderately low heat for 30 minutes, skimming occasionally. Remove from heat. Use a slotted spoon to remove about 1 cup of cooked vegetables from the soup. Place in bowl of food processor or blender and purée. Return the puréed vegetables to the soup. Add the corn kernels and their milk and simmer for 10 minutes. Do not boil.

Strain the stock, reserving the vegetables. Transfer them to a food processor and purée until smooth, about 1 minute. Pour the stock and puréed vegetables into one of the large saucepans and add the corn kernels and their milk. Season with the salt. Simmer until corn is just tender, about 5 minutes. Taste for seasoning and add freshly ground black pepper. Add the chopped scallions.

Yield: 6–8 servings

• SUMMER SOUP •

This delicious soup, tart from the sorrel and sweet from the corn, was put together from leftovers and what happened to be in the refrigerator and in the garden. It is so good that it has become a standard at our house. Serve it hot or at room temperature.

6 cups water
1 vegetable bouillon cube
6 small red potatoes, cut into small cubes
2 large leeks, cut into thin rounds
1 medium zucchini, diced into small pieces
½ pound sorrel leaves, finely chopped
2 cups fresh, cooked, or frozen corn kernels (about 4 ears of corn)

1 large ripe tomato, skinned and chopped fine (optional)
½ to ¾ pound skinless, boneless salmon fillet (Mine was already cooked, but you can use uncooked or you can leave it out.)
Salt to taste
Freshly ground black pepper to taste
A few sprigs of fresh dill

In a large soup pot, bring the water to a boil and add the vegetable bouillon cube. Stir to dissolve and reduce heat to a simmer. Add the potatoes and leeks. Stir and simmer for 15 minutes. Add the zucchini and sorrel leaves. Stir and simmer 10 minutes more. Add the corn kernels and tomato. Simmer 5 minutes more. Flake the cooked salmon into small pieces. If you are using uncooked salmon add to soup in one piece and flake with a fork after it has cooked through. Add salmon, heat through or cook 5 to 10 minutes longer until fish is done. Season to taste with salt and pepper. Garnish with fresh dill and serve.

Yield: 6 servings

Corn on the Table

Breakfasts, Main Dishes,
Pastas, Stews, Polentas

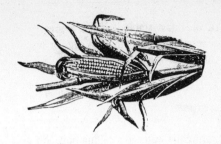

Fried mush came along in the fall, after the first harvest of winter corn and before the pancake season set in, and again in the spring when the batter pitcher was washed and put away. Fried mush for breakfast followed a preceding supper of mush and milk. My mother made her mush by sifting yellow corn meal, fresh from the mill, into an iron kettle of boiling salted water; with one hand she sifted the meal while with the other she stirred it with a wooden spoon. It was then drawn to the back of the stove to bubble and sputter and spurt for an hour or longer—and woe to you if it happened to spurt onto bare hand or arm while stirring.

Whatever mush was left over after supper was packed into a greased bread tin. In the morning this was sliced and fried in hot fat, and eaten with butter and syrup.

—Della T. Lutes, The Country Kitchen

◆ BREAKFAST CORN GRITS ◆

These are a Southern breakfast staple and are a great soluble-fiber alternative to oatmeal or your usual cereal. Serve them with eggs or on their own (sprinkled with toasted pumpkin or sunflower seeds).

5 cups water
1 cup white or yellow corn grits

½ teaspoon salt

In a heavy saucepan, bring the water to a rolling boil. Stir grits into the boiling water and when water returns to the boil, reduce heat to a simmer. Cook over low heat for 15 to 20 minutes, stirring occasionally. When grits have thickened, remove from heat and let stand a few minutes to thicken more. The longer they stand the thicker they get. Serve hot, with milk, brown sugar, maple syrup, toasted nuts or seeds, or your favorite jam.

Yield: 6 servings

Variation: For fried grits, pour the hot grits into a shallow loaf pan and let cool. Cut into serving-size pieces and fry in butter or margarine until golden brown on both sides. Serve with any cane sugar or maple syrup.

◆ COUCHE-COUCHE ◆

This Cajun cornmeal mush is a simple but delicious breakfast favorite. It is traditionally served with hot milk and cane syrup.

2 cups yellow cornmeal
1½ teaspoons salt
1 tablespoon baking powder

1½ cups hot water
¼ cup vegetable oil

In a large bowl, combine the cornmeal, salt, and baking powder. Slowly stir in the water and blend well.

Heat the oil in a heavy skillet until very hot. Pour in the cornmeal mixture and cook over high heat, without stirring, until a crust forms on the bottom, about 5 minutes. Now turn mixture over with a spatula, one load at a time. Stir well to break up the crust. Reduce the heat to low, and cook for 5 to 10 minutes more, stirring occasionally. The finished couche-couche should be lumpy and still a little moist but with bits of crispy crust throughout.

Serve in bowls with milk and your favorite syrup or preserves.

Yield: 6 servings

• FANCY GRITS CASSEROLE •

Even people who say they don't like grits love this casserole. Serve it with any meat or chicken dish or serve it for lunch with a big green salad.

6 cups water
2 teaspoons salt
1½ cups corn grits
1 stick butter
8 ounces sharp cheddar cheese, grated
2 to 3 garlic cloves, pressed

½ teaspoon cayenne
Dash of Tabasco
3 eggs
1½ cups milk
Freshly grated Parmesan cheese

Preheat oven to 350° F. Rub the insides of a 2-quart casserole with butter.

Bring water to a boil in a large saucepan. Stir the grits into the boiling water, stirring constantly until they are completely mixed. Cook, stirring, until thickened but still of a pourable consistency (about 15 minutes). Remove from heat and stir in the butter, cheddar cheese, garlic, cayenne, and Tabasco. In a separate bowl, beat the eggs together with the milk; then stir into the grits mixture. Pour the grits into the casserole. (You can prepare ahead up to this point. Refrigerate for as long as a day, then bake.)

Bake the casserole for 50 to 60 minutes. Remove from the oven, sprinkle with Parmesan cheese, and bake for 10 minutes longer.

Yield: 6 servings

◆ SALMON WITH CORN, LEEKS, AND TOMATOES ◆

3 tablespoons olive oil
4 boneless salmon fillets (about 2½
    pounds)
Salt to taste
Freshly ground black pepper to taste
4 small leeks, cut lengthwise in half and
    then finely chopped
3 large ripe tomatoes, peeled, seeded, and
    chopped

4 cups fresh corn kernels (about 8 ears of
    corn)
Salt to taste
Freshly ground black pepper to taste
Juice of ½ lemon
2 tablespoons fresh parsley, chopped

Heat 2 tablespoons of the oil in a nonstick skillet over moderately high heat until very hot and add the salmon pieces, skin side down. Cook for 3 minutes and turn over with a spatula. Cook for 3 minutes longer and remove to a platter. Peel away the burnt skin and discard. Season the fish fillets with salt and pepper. Add the remaining oil to the skillet. Add the leeks and cook, stirring, for five minutes, then add the tomatoes, corn kernels, salt, pepper, and lemon juice. Cook 5 minutes longer. Taste for seasoning and adjust. Divide the mixture among four plates, then place salmon over the corn mixture and sprinkle with parsley before serving.

   Yield: 4 servings

Note: If you prefer, grill the salmon pieces over hot coals.

◆ GRILLED TUNA WITH CORN SALSA ◆

¼ cup dry white wine
2 tablespoons virgin olive oil
2 teaspoons shallots, coarsely chopped
1 teaspoon garlic, coarsely chopped
½ teaspoon salt
½ teaspoon crushed black peppercorns
4 fresh tuna steaks, about 6 ounces each
3 ears fresh corn
3 large ripe tomatoes
1 large Spanish onion

3 tablespoons olive oil
6 scallions, finely chopped, including
    green parts
2 tablespoons finely chopped fresh
    coriander
¼ cup fresh lime juice
1 teaspoon salt
½ teaspoon freshly ground black pepper
¼ teaspoon cayenne, or to taste

In a shallow dish large enough to hold the tuna steaks, combine the wine, olive oil, shallots, garlic, salt, and peppercorns. Mix well and add the tuna steaks, turning them over in the marinade several times to coat well. Let stand at room temperature while you prepare corn salsa.

Start coals in outdoor grill or preheat broiler. Pull down green outer leaves of corn and remove as much of the silk as possible. Wrap green leaves back around the corn and soak in cold water for 5 minutes. Cut tomatoes into slices about ½ inch thick. Peel the onion and cut into ½-inch slices. When coals are hot, place the corn on grill. Brush tomato and onion slices with olive oil and grill them a few minutes on each side, until they just begin to sear. Remove to a platter to cool. Grill corn for 10 to 15 minutes, turning the ears occasionally. Remove the platter to cool. When vegetables are cool enough to handle, chop the tomatoes and onion and place into a bowl. Cut corn kernels away from the ears and add to tomatoes. Add the scallions, coriander, lime juice, salt, black pepper, and cayenne. Add the remaining olive oil. Mix well and taste for seasoning. Add more hot pepper if you like. Cover and let stand while you cook the tuna.

Remove fish from the marinade, reserving the marinade, and place on hot grill or in broiler and cook, allowing 10 minutes for every 1-inch thickness of fish. Turn fish over at midpoint.

Place marinade in a small saucepan and bring to a boil. Reduce heat and simmer for 3 minutes, remove from heat, and stir into the corn salsa.

Serve fish as soon as it is done with a dollop of salsa on top. Pass the remaining salsa at the table.

Yield: 4 servings

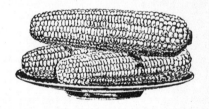

◆ MAQUECHOUX SHRIMP ◆

Many recipes for maquechoux call for butter and heavy cream, but to my taste olive oil and chicken stock deliver a lighter, fresher taste. You may adjust the fiery seasonings according to your taste, but remember that what makes this dish so pleasing is the contrast between the sweetness of the corn and the heat from the peppers.

1 pound medium shrimp
6 ears fresh sweet corn (substitute 1 package frozen corn kernels in the winter)
3 tablespoons olive oil
1 large onion, chopped
2 medium green peppers, seeded and chopped
1 large red pepper, seeded and chopped
1 large jalapeño pepper, seeded and chopped

½ cup strong chicken stock (dissolved bouillon cube is fine)
½ cup chopped parsley
½ teaspoon freshly ground black pepper
¼ teaspoon cayenne
Dash Tabasco or other hot pepper sauce (optional)
Salt if necessary

Peel, devein, and wash the shrimp. Dry on paper toweling and set aside. Shuck the corn and cut away the corn kernels with a small sharp knife. Scrape each cob with a dull butter knife to extract as much of the milky liquid as possible. You should end up with 3½ to 4 cups of corn kernels.

In a large skillet or sauté pan, heat the oil over medium heat and sauté the onion and all the peppers until softened, about 10 minutes. Stir in the shrimp and cook about 5 minutes, until shrimp turns pink. Add the corn, chicken stock, parsley, and all the seasonings and cook over high heat until heated through. Taste and adjust seasonings.

Serve in deep bowls, accompanied by crusty bread and a platter of sliced ripe tomatoes.

Yield: 4 servings

Note: To increase the number of servings, increase the amount of shrimp and corn: 1½ pounds shrimp and 9 ears of corn for 6 servings; 2 pounds shrimp and 12 ears corn for 8 servings.

• MAQUECHOUX CHICKEN •

8 ears of sweet corn
2 small chickens (about 3 pounds each),
   cut into pieces
4 tablespoons corn or other vegetable oil
2 large onions, chopped
2 green bell peppers, seeded and chopped
3 large ripe tomatoes, peeled and chopped
A large handful of fresh basil, chopped

A large handful of fresh parsley, chopped
½ teaspoon fresh thyme leaves (half that
   amount if dried)
1 teaspoon salt, or to taste
½ teaspoon freshly ground black pepper
¼ teaspoon cayenne, or more to taste
Dash of Tabasco

Shuck the corn and cut away the kernels. Scrape the cobs to extract all the milky liquid. You should have about 3½ to 4 cups of corn kernels.

Pick over the chicken pieces to remove all excess fat. Wash and dry on paper towels.

Heat the oil in a large, heavy skillet or sauté pan. When it is very hot, add the chicken pieces and cook them until they start to turn a golden brown. Turn them frequently with kitchen tongs. Cook the breast for 10 to 12 minutes, and the dark meat about 20 minutes. Remove chicken pieces to a large platter and reserve.

Pour out all but 2 tablespoons of fat and add the onions and peppers. Cook, stirring, for about 10 minutes until the onions become slightly translucent. Add the tomatoes (with all their juices), basil, parsley, and thyme. Simmer together for about 5 minutes, then add chicken pieces and any juices that have accumulated, salt, black pepper, cayenne, and Tabasco. Cook over gentle heat for 10 to 15 minutes, until chicken is fully cooked through. Add the corn kernels and heat through. Taste and adjust seasonings.

Serve in large soup bowls with crusty French bread.

Yield: 6 servings

Add corn kernels to your favorite foods. Whether you use cooked kernels from left-over corn on the cob, or freshly cut corn kernels from a handful of ears, or frozen kernels from your freezer, try adding them to the following:
- *your favorite chili recipe*
- *gazpacho*
- *scrambled eggs*
- *your favorite pancake batter*
- *any green salad*
- *spaghetti sauce*
- *vegetable stir-fry dishes*
- *meat loaf*

• LINGUINE WITH CORN AND CLAMS •

This is my variation on the classic linguine with clam sauce—it is always a hit.

3 to 4 dozen littleneck clams
3 tablespoons olive oil
4 garlic cloves, finely chopped
6 scallions, finely chopped
1 teaspoon dried red pepper flakes (or to taste)

2 tablespoons parsley, chopped
16 ounces fresh or dried linguine
2 cups fresh corn kernels (about 4 ears of corn)
Freshly ground black pepper to taste
Freshly grated Parmesan cheese

Scrub the clams under cold running water and place them in a large pot with ½ cup water. Cover the pot and place it over high heat to steam open the clams. Shake the pot from time to time to move the clams around. As the clams start to pop open, remove them with tongs to a large bowl. Some clams take longer than others to open, but if there are some that don't open at all, discard them. While the clams are cooling, strain the clam broth through a paper coffee filter or several thicknesses of cheesecloth. When clams are cool enough to handle, remove clams from shells and set aside. Discard the shells.

Put 4 to 6 quarts of water in a large pot to boil.

Place olive oil, chopped garlic, scallions, and red pepper flakes in a large sauté pan and cook over very low heat for about 10 minutes. Do not let the garlic or scallions brown. Add the reserved, strained clam broth and parsley.

Cook linguine until almost done and drain but reserve about 1 cup of the cooking water. Do not overcook as it will continue cooking in the sauce. Add linguine, corn kernels, and reserved clams to the sauce in sauté pan. Toss and mix well and cook over medium heat until everything is heated through and sauce has thickened slightly. If too dry, add a little of the reserved cooking water. Taste for seasoning and add freshly grated black pepper. Serve in large warmed soup bowls. Pass freshly grated Parmesan cheese.

Yield: 4–6 servings

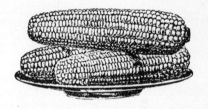

• UNCOOKED TOMATO-CORN SAUCE
FOR HOT PASTA •

This is my variation of a well-known classic summer dish. Ripe tomatoes, corn kernels, basil, and garlic are marinated in olive oil. Hot spaghetti is mixed into the uncooked sauce to impart its own heat. This is a simple, delicious dish that demands the finest, freshest ingredients. The spaghetti is eaten warm or at room temperature.

4–5 large ripe tomatoes
1½ cups cooked fresh corn kernels*
  (about 3 ears of corn)
2–3 garlic cloves, peeled and smashed
⅓ cup roughly chopped fresh basil leaves
⅓ cup roughly chopped Italian parsley

⅓ cup extra virgin olive oil
Salt to taste
Freshly ground black pepper to taste
1 pound thin spaghetti or spaghettini
Freshly grated Parmesan cheese

Prepare tomatoes about 1 hour before serving. Wash tomatoes, cut in half, and remove seeds. Chop tomato halves into small cubes and place in a serving bowl large enough to hold the spaghetti. Add the corn kernels, the smashed garlic cloves, basil, and parsley. Pour in olive oil and stir. Add salt and freshly ground black pepper to taste. Cover with plastic wrap and let stand until spaghetti is cooked.

Cook spaghetti, drain, and immediately toss with tomato-corn sauce. Serve immediately with lots of freshly grated Parmesan cheese.

Yield: 4 servings

Note: Remove the garlic cloves before serving if you wish.

*If you have very fresh corn, cut the kernels from the cob and add them to the tomatoes without cooking them. They will be sweet, crunchy, and delicious.

• FISH AND SCALLOP STEW WITH CORN •

1 pound monkfish
1 pound bay scallops or sea scallops cut in
    half
½ cup flour
½ teaspoon salt
½ teaspoon freshly ground black pepper
¼ teaspoon cayenne
½ cup vegetable oil
4 tablespoons butter

3 garlic cloves, finely minced
1 leek, finely sliced
¾ cup dry white wine
¾ cup fish stock or clam juice
1½ cups fresh corn kernels (about 3 ears
    of corn)
2 large ripe tomatoes, peeled, seeded, and
    chopped (about 1½ cups)
¾ cup fresh basil, finely shredded

Cut the monkfish into pieces roughly the size of the scallops. Mix together the flour, salt, black pepper, and cayenne. Dust the monkfish and scallops with the seasoned flour.

Heat the vegetable oil in a skillet or sauté pan and add the seafood in a single layer. Cook until just turning golden brown, about 1½ minutes, turn and cook another 1½ minutes. Remove to a paper towel to drain and finish cooking the rest of the fish and scallops.

Discard the cooking oil and wipe out skillet or sauté pan. Heat the butter until it sizzles and add garlic and leek. Cook over medium heat, stirring constantly, for about 1 minute. Do not let the garlic burn. Add the wine, increase heat to high, and cook until wine is reduced by half. Add fish stock or clam juice, corn, tomatoes, and basil. Cook, stirring, for 5 minutes. Add the monkfish and scallops and heat through. Serve in shallow bowls.

Yield: 6 servings

◆ HOPI CORN STEW WITH BLUE CORN DUMPLINGS ◆

My friend Claudia Jessup, who lives and writes in Santa Fe, sent me this recipe. It is easy and delicious.

1 pound ground lamb or beef*
1 tablespoon vegetable oil
2 cups fresh corn kernels (about 4 ears of corn)
1 green pepper, seeded and finely chopped
1 red pepper, seeded and finely chopped

1 cup summer squash or zucchini, cubed
Salt to taste
Freshly ground black pepper to taste
1 tablespoon coarse red chile powder (optional)
1 tablespoon whole-wheat flour

Fry meat in vegetable oil until brown. Add rest of ingredients except flour and cover with water. Simmer until vegetables are nearly tender, about 5 minutes. Mix 2 table-spoons cooking water with whole-wheat flour and return to stew. Simmer 5 more minutes, stirring. Add corn dumplings, if desired.

Yield: 6 servings

Corn has the macabre distinction of being one of the few documented ingredients of cannibal cuisine. The Aztec dish called "tlacatlaolli" was a kind of stew that called for Aztec as well as maize.

---

*The original recipe calls for ground goat meat.

◆ BLUE CORN DUMPLINGS ◆

1 cup blue cornmeal (use white if blue is
    unavailable)
2 teaspoons baking powder

1 teaspoon salt
1 teaspoon bacon drippings or shortening
⅓ to ½ cup milk

Sift dry ingredients. Add bacon drippings or cut in shortening and add enough milk to make a drop batter. Drop by spoonfuls on top of stew. Cover kettle and steam dumplings 15 minutes before lifting cover. Stew should keep bubbling.

Yield: 6 servings

A famous recipe for burgoo printed in the Louisville Courier-Journal calls for 800 pounds of beef, 200 pounds of fowl, 168 gallons canned tomatoes, 350 pounds cabbage, 6 bushels onions, 85 gallons tomato puree, 24 gallons carrots, 36 gallons canned corn, 1,800 pounds potatoes, 2 pounds red pepper, ½ pound black pepper, 20 pounds salt, 8 ounces Angostura bitters, 1 pint Worcestershire sauce, ½ pound curry powder, 3 quarts tomato catsup, and 2 quarts sherry. It is meant to serve 5,000 people.

This popular dish used to include all sorts of wild game—everything from squirrel to opossum. It is traditionally served at huge political rallies to hundreds of hungry people at a time. Naturally enough, this is a great party dish. Make it ahead and enjoy yourself.

2 pounds beef shank (bone in)
½ pound lamb
1 medium-size chicken (3–4 pounds), cut into pieces
4 quarts water, or more if needed
Salt to taste
Freshly ground black pepper to taste
1 dried red chile pepper or 1 teaspoon red pepper flakes
3 large potatoes, peeled and diced
2 cups diced onions

2 cups fresh or frozen lima beans
3 carrots, diced
2 green peppers, seeded and diced
3 cups fresh or frozen corn kernels cut off the cob (about 6 ears of corn)
2 cups okra, sliced into thin rings (use frozen if fresh not available)
1 28-ounce can tomatoes
1 clove garlic, peeled and smashed
1 cup minced parsley

Place the beef, lamb, and chicken in a large heavy pot with a tightly fitting lid. Add water, salt, and black and red pepper. Bring slowly to a boil, reduce to a bare simmer, and cook, covered, for 2 hours.

Add potatoes and onions; let simmer for 10 minutes. Add lima beans, carrots, and green peppers. Simmer 10 minutes longer. Add corn and simmer for 2 hours or until mixture is very thick. Watch carefully and stir frequently so that mixture doesn't stick. Add more water as necessary. At the end of 2 hours add okra, tomatoes, and garlic and let simmer for another 1½ hours. The total cooking time should be approximately 7 hours. The final soup or stew should be thick and the flavors should be very well blended. Stir in parsley just before serving.

Serve with any corn bread or corn pone.

Yield: 8–20 servings

Whole-kernel hominy, nixtamal, posole, and samp are all the same thing: dried corn kernels treated with lime.

Hominy and grits are made from mature (hard) corn kernels. Whole kernels soaked in a solution of water and lye to remove the outer hulls or husks become hominy; when hominy is dried and coarsely ground, it becomes grits.

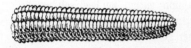

• CAROL'S POSOLE •

This recipe comes directly from one of Santa Fe's great cooks. It can be served as a main dish or side dish or as part of a buffet table.

1 boneless pork roast (about 4 pounds) trimmed of fat and cut into 1-inch chunks
8 cups water
1 small onion, stuck with 2 cloves
2 cloves garlic, unpeeled
1 bay leaf
1 teaspoon salt
½ teaspoon whole cumin seed
1 dried red chile pepper
1 package (20 ounces) dry posole
4 medium onions, chopped
6 cloves garlic, minced

3 tablespoons olive oil
1 tablespoon coarse red chile powder (or to taste)*
1 teaspoon dried oregano
½ teaspoon freshly ground black pepper
½ teaspoon ground cumin
½ teaspoon ground cloves
2 large (35-ounce) cans whole tomatoes, chopped into pieces
1 cup canned green chilies, chopped
2 whole jalapeño peppers (fresh or canned), chopped

Place the pork, water, onion, garlic, bay leaf, salt, cumin seed, and dried chili pepper in a large pot and bring to a boil. There will be a lot of scum. Skim off the foam, reduce heat, and simmer gently over low heat for 1 hour. Remove from heat and allow to cool. Strain the broth, skim off as much fat as possible, and reserve. Shred

*Everyone has his or her own version of how much chile powder to use. Chile powder comes in mild, medium, and hot—use whatever you prefer.

the meat by hand into bite-size pieces. (This can be done a day or two ahead.)

Place posole and enough water to cover it in a separate saucepan. Bring water to a boil, then reduce heat and simmer until it pops, about 1½ hours; drain. (This can be done a day ahead.)

In a large heavy dutch oven, sauté the onions and garlic in the olive oil until they soften and turn translucent. Do not burn. Add the chile powder, oregano, black pepper, cumin, and cloves and cook, stirring, for 1 minute. Add the pork, cooked posole, tomatoes, chilies, jalapeño peppers, and the reserved broth from the pork. Simmer over low heat for 1 to 1½ hours. The meat and hominy should be very tender and the broth should be thickened slightly. If the stew seems too dry (there should be some broth for every serving when it is done), add more water as needed.

Serve posole in deep bowls and pass the salsa cruda.

Yield: 10–12 servings

Note: If you are unable to buy dried posole, substitute 4 cups canned white or yellow hominy. Add it as you would the cooked posole.

In the old plain-spoken days, posole used to be called "hog and hominy." A poor man's posole has a lot of hominy and just a bit of pork to give it taste. A rich man's posole, or a feast-day posole, has lots and lots of stewed pork meat cheering up the hominy.

• SALSA CRUDA •

1½ cups chopped tomato pulp (either
   fresh tomatoes, peeled, seeded, and
   chopped or canned tomatoes, drained
   and chopped)
1 clove garlic
1 small red onion, finely chopped
1 fresh or canned jalapeño pepper,
   seeded, deveined, and minced
   (optional)

3 canned green chilies, chopped fine
1 tablespoon finely chopped coriander
1 teaspoon olive oil
Juice of 1 lime
Salt to taste
Freshly ground black pepper to taste

Put the chopped tomatoes into a small bowl and press the garlic clove through a garlic press into the tomatoes. Stir in the onion, jalapeño, green chilies, coriander, olive oil, and lime juice. Mix well and season with salt and pepper to taste. You can add more spicy hotness by adding more jalapeños.

◆ BASIC POLENTA ◆

The most basic polenta is nothing but water, salt, and cornmeal. If you want to make basic polenta, omit the other ingredients. But the simple addition of butter and garlic to the cooking water transforms an ordinary dish of mush into something quite tasty and extraordinary. As for the method of making polenta, there are various approaches. Some cooks like to make a paste with the cornmeal and cold water before stirring into the hot water; some insist on the classical method of stirring a fine stream of cornmeal into violently boiling water. The method described below is easy, lump-free, and you don't have to stand over boiling water.

7 cups water
1 teaspoon salt
3 tablespoons butter

3 cloves garlic, crushed
2 cups coarsely ground cornmeal

Bring the water to a boil in a large, heavy pot. (The water should not come more than halfway up the sides of the pot.) Turn off the heat. Stir in salt, butter, and garlic. Then stir in cornmeal, pouring it in a fine, steady stream as you stir. Place the pot over medium-high heat and continue stirring as the cornmeal boils and thickens. Make sure to use a long-handled wooden spoon and to stand back from the pot so the bubbles don't explode in your face. As the cornmeal thickens, the boiling mass might get violent. Simply turn off the heat and keep stirring. When it has calmed down, turn up the heat and continue cooking until done. The total cooking time is usually 15 to 20 minutes. The polenta is done when it forms a very thick mass and starts to pull away from the sides of the pot as you stir. Serve soft polenta plain with a little butter and freshly grated Parmesan cheese; with your favorite tomato or pasta sauce; or with any dish that makes its own gravy, like pot roast or stew. You can serve it on its own, like a bowl of pasta, or as a side dish to replace any other starchy dish.

Yield: 6–8 servings

Variation: For an even more flavorful polenta, replace the water with homemade chicken or beef broth.

• FRIED POLENTA •

Make polenta as described above, then pour either into an oiled 9 × 5 × 3-inch loaf pan or 9 × 12-inch roasting pan and cover with plastic wrap and refrigerate for several hours or overnight. (The dimensions of both the loaf pan and the roasting pan are not critical; use any pans you have that are about that size.) Cut polenta either into ½-inch slices or into squares, triangles, or even circles, using a cookie cutter. Heat about 2 tablespoons olive oil or olive oil mixed with butter in a large skillet and fry the polenta pieces until golden brown on both sides.

• GRILLED POLENTA •

Prepare polenta as for fried polenta. Brush polenta pieces with olive oil on each side and grill over hot coals or under a broiler for about two minutes on each side, until golden brown.

• POLENTA WITH MUSHROOMS •

The smooth, creamy texture of polenta goes wonderfully well with the rich, woodsy taste of mushrooms.

Basic Polenta (page 75)
1 cup very hot water
1 ounce dried porcini mushrooms
¼ pound fresh shiitake mushrooms
2 tablespoons olive oil
1 medium onion, finely chopped
2 cloves garlic, finely minced
2 cups Italian-style canned tomatoes,
 drained and chopped

1 teaspoon fresh thyme leaves (or ½
 teaspoon dried)
2 tablespoons chopped parsley
Salt to taste
Freshly ground black pepper to taste
2 tablespoons olive oil
½ cup freshly grated Parmesan cheese

Prepare polenta (*see* page 75) and pour into oiled loaf pan or roasting pan. Cover and refrigerate for several hours. (This can be done a day in advance.)

In a mixing bowl, pour the hot water over the dried mushrooms and let stand for 15 minutes. Strain the mushrooms and strain the mushroom water through a paper coffee filter or several layers of cheesecloth. Reserve the strained water. Rinse the mushrooms under cold running water to wash away any grit. Cut away and discard the stems. Chop the mushrooms into ¼-inch pieces. Wipe shiitake mushrooms with a damp cloth. Cut away and discard the stems and cut mushrooms into ¼-inch slices.

In a skillet or sauté pan, heat the olive oil, add onion and garlic. Cook, stirring, over medium heat for 3 to 5 minutes. Do not let garlic brown. Add the tomatoes, thyme, parsley, and the liquid from the mushrooms. Simmer over medium heat for 15 minutes. Add the mushrooms, salt, and freshly ground black pepper, and simmer 10 minutes longer.

Preheat oven to 425° F.

Cut polenta into ½-inch slices or into 2½-inch squares and arrange on an oiled baking sheet. Brush polenta with olive oil, sprinkle with Parmesan cheese, and bake for 15 to 20 minutes, until the cheese has turned golden brown.

Serve the polenta with the mushroom sauce on top. Pass additional freshly grated Parmesan cheese if desired.

Yield: 6 servings

Note: Polenta slices may be fried in oil or butter or grilled instead of baking. See page 77 for instructions.

• POLENTA LASAGNA •

Basic Polenta (page 75)
½ cup freshly grated Parmesan cheese
2 tablespoons olive oil
1 medium onion, finely chopped
1 clove garlic, crushed
1 carrot, finely chopped
1 celery stalk, finely chopped
½ pound ground round or sirloin
1 can (28 ounces) Italian-style peeled tomatoes, roughly chopped

1 tablespoon salt
½ teaspoon sugar
½ teaspoon dried red pepper flakes
¼ teaspoon freshly ground black pepper
½ pound skim-milk mozzarella cheese, finely diced
½ cup freshly grated Parmesan cheese
½ cup freshly grated Pecorino Romano cheese
2 tablespoons butter

Prepare the polenta according to the directions on page 75. While the polenta is still hot, stir in ½ cup freshly grated Parmesan cheese. Pour the polenta into an oiled 17 × 12-inch jellyroll pan, cover with plastic wrap, and cool. Polenta can stay in refrigerator up to two days.

In a large saucepan, heat the oil, add the onion, and cook over moderate heat until softened and translucent, 3 to 5 minutes. Add the garlic, carrot, and celery stalk and cook five minutes longer. Add the ground beef and cook, stirring, until meat has lost all its pink color. Add tomatoes with their juice, salt, sugar, red pepper flakes, and black pepper. Simmer, stirring occasionally, until the sauce thickens, about 30 minutes. The tomato sauce can be made several days ahead and kept refrigerated.

Grease a lasagna pan with olive oil or butter. Pour a thin layer of tomato sauce on the bottom. Cut a layer of polenta to fit into the lasagna pan. This does not have to be in one piece but can be patched together. Sprinkle a layer of mozzarella cheese over the polenta, cover with another layer of tomato sauce and sprinkle with Parmesan and Pecorino Romano. Cover with another layer of polenta, mozzarella, tomato sauce, Parmesan, and Pecorino Romano, in that order. Dot the surface with butter. This can be assembled the day before and kept in the refigerator. Bring to room temperature before baking.

Preheat oven to 375° F.

Bake the polenta for 25 to 30 minutes. The cheese should be melted and crusty on top. Remove from the oven and let stand for 5 to 10 minutes before serving.

Yield: 6 servings

Note: For a vegetarian meal, omit the meat and make the tomato sauce without it in exactly the same way. Or, add ½ to 1 pound mushrooms and sauté the mushrooms with the other vegetables before adding the tomatoes.

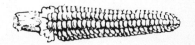

Corn from the Oven

Skillet Breads, Corn Breads, Spoon Bread, Muffins

Corn is the country's national vegetable. Johnny cake, dodgers, pone, hoecake, ashcake, fritters, hominy, spoon bread, Indian pudding, hasty pudding—all of these spell c-o-r-n to us in no uncertain terms.

—Nicholas P. Hardeman, Shucks, Shocks, and Hominy Blocks—
Corn as a Way of Life in Pioneer America

About Corn Breads and Muffins

Corn breads and muffins are among the easiest and most satisfying breads you can bake. They are so quick and so easy to make that you could have fresh hot corn bread or muffins with every meal and very little trouble on your part. This was in fact the case in many early American households.

I make most of my corn breads in a heavy black cast-iron skillet that measures 9 inches in diameter. (Ten or even 12 inches in diameter would be fine, too.) The skillet is always preheated in the oven with some butter or oil so that the corn bread batter goes into a hot, well-greased skillet. This method produces a bread that is crispy on the outside and light and moist inside. But cornbreads are nothing if not adaptable, so if you don't own a heavy skillet or pan, or have mixed up your batter and forgotten to preheat the skillet, go ahead and bake the bread in an unheated buttered or oiled skillet or baking pan. Any baking pan approximately 8 × 8 × 2 inches is suitable to use instead of the 9-inch skillet. You can bake any corn bread recipe (except for spoon bread) as muffins or corn sticks, or vice versa.

The recipes are adaptable in many other ways as well. Yellow, white, and blue cornmeal are all interchangeable—only do try to get the freshest stone-ground cornmeal, which you should keep refrigerated. If buttermilk is called for and you don't have any on hand, substitute an equal amount of plain low-fat yogurt; or milk (skim or regular) plus 1 tablespoon lemon juice. No lemon in the house? Skip it, the bread will still come out okay. You can leave out or increase the amount of sugar called for. The taste for sugar in corn bread is personal as well as regional. Northerners tend to like their corn breads sweet; Southerners never add sugar. You can add fresh herbs, a little bit of cheese, a handful of corn kernels, or some crumbled bacon bits to almost any corn bread recipe. If you are watching your cholesterol, substitute vegetable oil for butter, use two egg whites for every whole egg, substitute skim milk or buttermilk (very low in fat) for whole milk, and leave out any cheese.

Most of the recipes in this section can be made in about 30 minutes. You can turn any meal into a special occasion by serving hot corn bread fresh from the oven. And that is the way that corn breads are best: hot or warm, but served as soon as possible after they are baked. Corn breads are not great keepers, so if you have leftovers, turn to the recipe for corn bread stuffing or cush to see what can be done. Or do as our forefathers did: Crumble some stale corn bread into a soup bowl, pour in some milk (a little brown sugar is optional), and have yourself a great breakfast or snack.

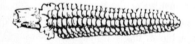

• BUTTERMILK CORN BREAD •

This delicious corn bread gets very crisp on the outside and remains moist inside.

2 tablespoons butter or vegetable oil
1½ cups buttermilk
2 large eggs
1 teaspoon salt

1 teaspoon baking powder
½ teaspoon baking soda
2 cups white cornmeal

Preheat oven to 450° F. Place the butter or vegetable oil in a heavy cast-iron skillet and put it in the oven to heat while you mix together the corn bread batter (this takes about 10 minutes).

In a large mixing bowl, whisk together the buttermilk and eggs. Stir in salt, baking powder, and baking soda. Stir in the cornmeal to make a batter. Remove the skillet from the oven and place on a padded surface. Swirl the oil or melted butter to coat the sides of the skillet. Pour the batter into the hot skillet and shake the skillet to smooth the batter. Bake for 20 minutes, until it turns a golden brown and edges recede from the sides of the pan. Cut into pie-shaped wedges and serve immediately.

Yield: 6–8 servings

• DROWNED CORN BREAD •

3 tablespoons butter or margarine
1 cup buttermilk
2 eggs, well beaten
½ cup sugar
1½ cups cornmeal

½ cup flour
1 teaspoon baking soda
¼ teaspoon salt
1 cup milk or half-and-half

Preheat oven to 400° F. Place the butter or margarine in a heavy cast-iron skillet and place the skillet in the oven for at least 10 minutes.

In a large bowl, whisk together the buttermilk, eggs, and sugar. Stir in the cornmeal, flour, baking soda, and salt. Remove the skillet from the oven and place on a padded surface. Swirl the melted butter to coat the sides of the skillet. Pour the batter into the hot pan. Smooth the batter with a wooden spoon and pour the milk or half-and-half over it. Do not stir. Bake at 400° F. for 25 to 30 minutes. The bread will be topped with a yellow custard. Cut into pie-shaped wedges and serve immediately.

Yield: 6 servings

All corn bread is delicate and crumbly when warm, so it helps to use a pie or cake server when removing it from the pan.

◆ BLUE-CORN SKILLET BREAD ◆

2 tablespoons butter
1½ cups buttermilk
1 large egg
½ cup vegetable oil
2 tablespoons sugar
2 teaspoons baking powder

½ teaspoon baking soda
½ teaspoon salt
1 cup blue cornmeal
⅓ cup whole-wheat flour
⅔ cup all-purpose white flour

Preheat oven to 400° F. Place the butter in a heavy cast-iron skillet and put the skillet in the oven for at least 10 minutes.

In a bowl, whisk together the buttermilk, egg, and vegetable oil. Stir in the sugar, baking powder, baking soda, and salt. Stir in the cornmeal and flours to make a batter. Remove the skillet from the oven and place on a padded surface. Swirl the melted butter to coat the sides of the skillet. Pour the batter into the skillet. Bake corn bread for 25 to 30 minutes, until firm and springy to the touch and lightly browned. Cut into wedges and serve hot.

Yield: 6 servings

Variation: Add ¾ cup fresh corn kernels (1-2 ears of corn) to batter.

◆ SOUTHERN CORN BREAD ◆

Corn bread pure and simple. This is very crumbly because it has no white flour in it at all. Serve it hot with lots of butter. Bake in a skillet or corn stick pan.

2 tablespoons butter or vegetable oil
1 cup buttermilk
1 large egg
1 teaspoon baking powder

½ teaspoon baking soda
¾ teaspoon salt
⅞ cup white cornmeal

Preheat oven to 425° F. Place butter or oil in heavy cast-iron skillet and place skillet in oven for 15 minutes.

In a bowl, whisk together the buttermilk and egg. Stir in baking powder, baking soda, and salt. Stir in the cornmeal. Remove the skillet from the oven and place on a padded surface. Swirl the melted butter to coat the sides of the skillet. Pour batter into hot skillet and bake for 20 to 25 minutes, until browned and crispy around the edges. Cut into wedges and serve hot.

Yield: 6 servings

◆ SUMMER CORN BREAD ◆

3 tablespoons butter
1½ cups milk
2 eggs
¼ cup vegetable oil
1 cup fresh corn kernels (about 2 ears of corn)

1 tablespoon fresh sage, finely minced
3 teaspoons baking powder
1 tablespoon sugar
1 teaspoon salt
¾ cup yellow cornmeal
½ cup all-purpose flour

Preheat oven to 400° F. Put butter in a heavy cast-iron skillet and place skillet in the oven for at least 10 minutes.

In a bowl, whisk together the milk, eggs, and vegetable oil. Stir in corn kernels, sage, baking powder, sugar, and salt. Stir in cornmeal and flour to make a batter. Remove the skillet from the oven and place on a padded surface. Swirl the melted butter to coat the sides of the skillet. Pour batter into hot skillet and bake for 30 to 35 minutes, until bread is golden and sides are crispy and pull away from the pan. Cut into wedges and serve hot or warm.

Yield: 6–8 servings

Pray, let me, an American, inform the gentleman, who seems ignorant of the matter, that Indian corn, take it for all in all, is one of the most agreeable and wholesome grains in the world and that johnny cake or hoe cake, hot from the fire is better than a Yorkshire muffin.

—*Benjamin Franklin, writing in the London Gazetteer, 1776, in defense of American corn, which the English regarded with disdain*

Laura always wondered why bread made of corn meal was called johnny-cake. It wasn't cake. Ma didn't know, unless the Northern soldiers called it johnny-cake because the people in the South, where they fought, ate so much of it. They called the Southern soldiers Johnny Rebs.

—*Laura Ingalls Wilder,* Little House in the Big Woods

◆ NOVA SCOTIA JOHNNYCAKE ◆

2 tablespoons butter
¾ cup buttermilk
⅓ cup maple syrup
¼ cup vegetable oil
2 large eggs

1 tablespoon baking powder
¾ teaspoon salt
1 cup all-purpose flour
1 cup white cornmeal

Preheat oven to 425° F. Put the butter in a heavy cast-iron skillet and place skillet in oven.

In a bowl, whisk together the buttermilk, maple syrup, vegetable oil, and eggs. Stir in baking powder and salt. Stir in flour and cornmeal and mix well. Remove the skillet from the oven and place on a padded surface. Pour batter into hot skillet and bake for 20 to 25 minutes, until top is golden and sides pull away from the pan. Cut into wedges and serve warm.

Yield: 6–8 servings

Variation: Add 1 cup of blueberries to the batter before baking.

• SHAKER CORN STICKS •

Shaker cooking is simple, practical, wholesome, and guaranteed to please the over-stimulated modern palate. The Shakers, with their no-nonsense approach to life, invented clothespins and flat brooms and perfected these corn sticks.

1 cup buttermilk
1 large egg, beaten lightly
2 tablespoons vegetable oil
1 tablespoon sugar
½ teaspoon baking soda

½ teaspoon baking powder
½ teaspoon salt
½ cup all-purpose flour
1 cup white cornmeal★
Additional oil for brushing the molds

Preheat oven to 450° F. Rub cast-iron corn stick molds (these should be 5½ inches long) with vegetable oil and preheat them in hot oven for 10 minutes. They should be very hot.

In a large mixing bowl, whisk together the buttermilk, egg, and vegetable oil. Stir in sugar, baking soda, baking powder, and salt, then stir in flour and cornmeal to make a smooth batter. Remove hot molds from the oven and place them on a padded surface. Spoon the batter into the molds, filling them about half full. Bake for about 15 minutes or until corn sticks are golden brown. Slide corn sticks from mold. Serve warm with plenty of sweet butter.

Yield: about 14 corn sticks

◆ CARROT CORN BREAD ◆

This is a lovely, moist, sweetly delicate corn bread. Serve it with split pea soup and a salad for a perfect evening meal.

3 carrots, finely grated
2 eggs
4 tablespoons oil
2 cups buttermilk
¼ cup sugar (optional)

½ teaspoon salt
1 teaspoon baking soda
1 teaspoon baking powder
2 cups yellow cornmeal
1 tablespoon butter

Preheat oven to 450° F.

In a bowl, combine carrots, eggs, oil, and buttermilk. Mix with wooden spoon until well blended. Stir in sugar, salt, baking soda, and baking powder. Then stir in cornmeal and blend to make a batter. Melt the butter in a heavy cast-iron skillet and use a paper towel to distribute butter evenly over the inside of the skillet. Pour in batter and bake 25 to 30 minutes, until mixture shrinks away from the side of skillet. Let cool in skillet for 15 to 20 minutes before serving to firm up the bread; otherwise, serve like pudding from a large serving spoon.

Yield: 6–8 servings

Variation: Substitute 1 cup grated zucchini for the carrots.

◆ SAUSAGE-APPLE CORN BREAD ◆

1 pound breakfast sausage links
2 Granny Smith apples, peeled, cored,
*   and cut into thin slices*
1 cup milk
1 slightly beaten egg

2 tablespoons vegetable oil
4 teaspoons baking powder
2 tablespoons sugar
1 cup flour
1 cup yellow cornmeal

Preheat oven to 425° F.

Cut the sausage into bite-size pieces and fry until browned on all sides. Turn frequently to brown evenly and keep from burning. Arrange the apple slices and about ⅓ of the sausage in bottom of a well-greased cast-iron skillet. Stir the remaining sausage into the batter (*below*).

In a medium-size bowl, whisk together the milk, egg, and vegetable oil. Stir in the baking powder and sugar, then stir in flour and cornmeal to make a smooth batter. Fold in the remaining sausage. Pour the batter over the apple rings and sausage. Bake for 30 to 35 minutes, until top is browned and sides pull away from the pan. Cut into wedges and serve hot or warm.

Yield: 6–8 servings

• ROMANIAN CORN BREAD (MALAI) •

Corn is a staple in Romania and their cornbread is very similar to our own. This recipe is an unusual variation. The bread is leavened with yeast and dotted with bits of feta cheese.

1 tablespoon active dry yeast
¼ cup warm water
1¼ cups milk
3 tablespoons sugar
2¼ cups yellow cornmeal

¼ cup all-purpose flour
2 tablespoons butter
2 large eggs, beaten
1 cup crumbled feta cheese

In a small bowl, dissolve the yeast in the warm water. In a large mixing bowl combine milk and sugar. Stir in the dissolved yeast, then stir in the cornmeal and flour to make a batter. Cover with plastic wrap and let stand in a warm place for 30 minutes to let the batter rise.

Preheat oven to 350° F. Place the butter in a heavy cast-iron skillet or 9-inch-square pan and place in the oven.

In a small bowl, beat the eggs, then beat them into the batter. Fold in crumbled feta cheese. Remove the skillet from the oven and place on a padded surface. Swirl the melted butter to coat the sides of the skillet or pan. Pour the batter into the skillet and bake for 45 to 50 minutes, until it has puffed and is quite firm. Serve hot.

Yield: 6–8 servings

• WHOLE-WHEAT CORN BREAD •

This bread tastes delicious with lentil or black bean soup and makes a complete protein source when combined with either soup.

2¼ cups whole-wheat pastry flour
3½ cups cornmeal
1 teaspoon baking powder
1 teaspoon baking soda

1 teaspoon salt
¼ cup butter
1 cup honey
3 cups milk or buttermilk

Preheat oven to 325° F.

In a large bowl, sift together whole-wheat pastry flour, cornmeal, baking powder, baking soda, and salt. Melt the butter, stir in honey, then add milk. Stir the liquid ingredients into the flour mixture to make a wet batter. Pour into a greased 9 × 12-inch pan and bake at 325° F. for 1¼ hours. Cut into wedges and serve hot or warm.

Yield: 8–10 servings

Nothing is superior to brown bread for bone and tooth building. Baked beans, too, have a considerable supply of these lime salts and should be on everyone's table hot or cold twice a week.

—The Manifesto, *a Shaker periodical*

Researchers at Georgetown University Hospital have discovered that raw corn bran can help reduce serum cholesterol levels by 20%. And corn fiber is more plentiful and has fewer calories than other cereal fibers.

—Adweek, *November 7, 1988*

• BOSTON BROWN BREAD •

2 tablespoons butter or margarine
1 cup whole-wheat flour
1 cup rye flour
1 cup cornmeal
1½ teaspoons baking soda
1½ teaspoons baking powder
1 teaspoon salt

1 egg
2 tablespoons vegetable oil
¾ cup molasses
¼ cup honey
2 cups buttermilk
1 cup raisins, chopped

To make this bread, you will need two 1-pound coffee cans with their plastic lids, a large pot to hold the cans, and a steamer rack for the cans to stand on.

Grease the insides of the coffee cans and the lids with the butter or margarine and set aside.

In a large bowl, combine whole-wheat flour, rye flour, and cornmeal. Stir in baking soda, baking powder, and salt. In another bowl, beat the egg, then whisk in the oil, molasses, and honey. Add the molasses-honey mixture to the dry ingredients and stir well. Add buttermilk and raisins and beat until smooth. Spoon equal amounts of batter into the two greased coffee cans—they should be about two-thirds full. Put the lids on and set cans on rack in a large kettle. Pour in boiling water to come halfway up the cans. Cover kettle tightly and steam over a medium flame (keep the water at a gentle boil) for 2½ hours. Remove cans from kettle, remove lids, and turn upside down onto a clean surface. Slice into rounds. Serve warm or cold.

Yield: 2 loaves

• ANADAMA BREAD •

2 cups milk
1 cup water
4 tablespoons butter
1 cup white cornmeal
5–6 cups all-purpose flour (preferably
    unbleached)

½ cup molasses
2 tablespoons active dry yeast
1 tablespoon salt

In a medium saucepan, combine milk, water, and butter. Heat to boiling and remove from heat. Slowly stir in cornmeal and continue stirring until smooth. Pour
into a large mixing bowl and let stand until lukewarm. Stir in 1 cup of flour, molasses, yeast, and salt. Add up to 4 more cups of flour, stirring in 1 cup at a time.
Beat mixture with a wooden spoon until dough starts to stiffen and comes away from
the sides of the bowl. Turn the dough out onto a board and knead for ten minutes,
adding additional flour as necessary to make a smooth, elastic dough. Place the
dough in a greased bowl and cover with plastic wrap. Let rise in a warm place until
it doubles in size, about 1 to 1½ hours.

Punch down dough and divide it into 2 or 3 equal parts. Place in greased bread
pans (dough should fill pan halfway), cover with a clean towel, and let rise once
more until double in size, about 45 minutes to 1 hour.

Preheat oven to 375° F.

Bake for 50 minutes. Bread sounds hollow when tapped with fingers when it is
done. Remove from pan. Cool on racks.

Yield: 2 large or 3 medium loaves

• CORN WHEAT LOAF •

2 tablespoons active dry yeast
½ cup warm water
1 cup milk
2 large eggs
¼ cup honey or molasses

3 tablespoons vegetable oil
2 teaspoons salt
1 cup yellow cornmeal
2 cups whole-wheat flour, approximately

In a small bowl, sprinkle the yeast over the warm water and stir to dissolve. In a large mixing bowl combine milk, eggs, honey or molasses, and vegetable oil. Stir in yeast mixture, then stir in salt, cornmeal, and as much flour as you need to make a workable dough. Remove dough to a kneading board sprinkled with more flour and knead for 10 to 15 minutes, until dough is smooth and satiny. Place dough in a well-greased 9 × 5 × 3-inch loaf pan and let rise in a warm place until dough has doubled in size (2 to 3 hours).

Preheat oven to 375° F.

Bake for 40 to 45 minutes until loaf is well browned. Bread sounds hollow when tapped with fingers when it is done. Turn loaf out onto wire rack to cool.

Yield: 1 loaf

⋆ INDIAN PUDDING ⋆

5 cups milk
½ cup yellow cornmeal
½ cup unsulphured molasses
¼ cup sugar
1 teaspoon salt

½ teaspoon cinnamon
½ teaspoon ginger
¼ teaspoon nutmeg
¼ teaspoon allspice
¼ cup butter

Preheat oven to 300° F.

In a heavy saucepan or in the top of a double boiler heat 4 cups of milk until very hot, but do not boil. Reserve the remaining 1 cup of milk. In a large bowl, mix together the cornmeal, molasses, sugar, salt, cinnamon, ginger, nutmeg, and allspice. Whisk the scalded milk, a little at a time, into the cornmeal mixture until smooth. Stir in butter and return to saucepan or double boiler. Cook, stirring, over moderate heat for 3 to 5 minutes, until the mixture thickens.

Pour into a buttered, 1½- to 2-quart ovenproof baking dish. Bake for 1 hour, then pour remaining 1 cup of milk over top of pudding. Do not stir. Bake 3 hours more. Serve hot, warm, or chilled with heavy cream, ice cream, or hard sauce.

Yield: 6–8 servings

Variations:
1. Add ½ cup of raisins to the cornmeal mixture.
2. Peel, core, and slice 3 apples and place in bottom of buttered baking dish. Pour pudding mixture over the apples and proceed as above.

◆ CORNMEAL FOCCACIA
WITH ONION AND THYME LEAVES ◆

These individual pizza breads are completely beguiling and a delicious departure from ordinary breads. Serve them with soup or a bean salad to make a complete meal, or cut them in quarters and serve as hors d'oeuvres.

1 package active dry yeast
1 cup warm water
½ teaspoon sugar
2 cups all-purpose flour, plus additional
*   flour for kneading*
1 cup yellow cornmeal, plus cornmeal for
*   dusting the baking sheet*
1½ teaspoons salt

4 tablespoons olive oil
1 very large onion (1¼ pounds
*   approximately), minced*
4 tablespoons olive oil
2 teaspoons fresh thyme leaves (or ½
*   teaspoon dried thyme)*
2 teaspoons coarse sea salt

In a small bowl, combine the yeast, water, and sugar, and let stand about 5 minutes, until foamy.

In a large mixing bowl, combine the flour, cornmeal, and salt. Make a well in the center and pour in the yeast mixture, along with 3 tablespoons of olive oil. Mix with a wooden spoon until the mixture holds together, then remove to a floured surface and knead for about 10 minutes until dough is smooth and satiny. Rub the inside of a large bowl with remaining olive oil. Shape the dough into a ball and rub the surface with a little olive oil. Place in bowl, cover with plastic wrap, and let stand in a warm place until the dough has doubled in bulk, about 1½ hours.

In the meantime, gently cook the onion in 3 tablespoons of olive oil over low heat for 20 to 30 minutes, until it has softened and reduced in bulk by almost half. Remove from heat and stir in thyme leaves.

Punch down the dough, knead to release the bubbles, cover, and let rest for about 30 minutes.

Preheat oven to 425° F.

Divide the dough into 8 equal pieces. On a floured surface, roll out each piece to form a four-inch circle. Dust two baking sheets with cornmeal, and place the breads on the baking sheet 1 inch apart. Brush each bread with oil and spread a heaping teaspoon of cooked onions over the top. Sprinkle with coarse salt.

Bake 15 minutes, or until golden brown and crisp. Serve warm or at room temperature.

Yield: 8 foccacia

Variations:

1. Brush foccacia with olive oil, sprinkle with fresh rosemary needles and pitted Greek or Italian olives.

2. Brush foccacia with olive oil, sprinkle with finely minced fresh sage and coarse sea salt.

As for corn, it is so important in our diet that some of us feel we must have eaten it from the beginning of time. Indeed, I had a friend who insisted that corn originated in our mountains, and nothing would change his mind. One day I showed him an encyclopedia article on maize, which said flatly that American Indians developed corn. "It only proves," he said, "that those Indians were lost Georgians who somehow got to America, with corn in their pockets."

—George Papashvily writing about the food of Georgia and Armenia in
Russian Cooking

• SPOON BREAD •

2 tablespoons butter
1 cup cornmeal
3 cups milk
1 teaspoon salt

1 teaspoon baking powder
3 tablespoons butter
3 egg yolks
3 egg whites

Preheat oven to 400° F. Grease the bottom and sides of a 2-quart ovenproof casserole or soufflé dish with 2 tablespoons of butter.

In a large bowl, stir the cornmeal into 1 cup of milk until well mixed. Bring the other 2 cups of milk just to the boil and remove from heat. Stir salt, baking powder, and 3 tablespoons butter into hot milk. Slowly stir hot milk into the cold milk and cornmeal mixture. Return to saucepan and cook over a low flame, stirring constantly, until mixture has thickened. Remove from heat and let cool a little. Beat in the three egg yolks. Beat the egg whites until stiff peaks form, then fold into cornmeal mixture. Turn mixture out into the large greased casserole and bake for 45 to 50 minutes, or until golden brown and puffed. Serve immediately. You will need a large serving spoon to "spoon" soufflélike bread onto the plates.

Yield: 6 servings

Variations:

1. Add 3 tablespoons chopped scallions to the batter, before adding egg whites.

2. Fold in 1 cup corn kernels (about 2 ears of corn) and 2 tablespoons chopped jalapeño pepper, before adding egg whites.

3. Fold in ½ cup grated Parmesan, or any other grated cheese, before adding egg whites.

◆ CREAMY CORN BREAD WITH CHEESE AND CHILIES ◆

An American Southwest classic, this corn bread is a sure-fire winner.

2 tablespoons butter
⅔ cup milk
2 large eggs
6 tablespoons melted butter
1 teaspoon baking powder
½ teaspoon baking soda
1 teaspoon salt

Freshly ground black pepper to taste
1 cup yellow cornmeal
1 17-ounce can cream-style corn
2 4-ounce cans green chilies, drained and chopped
2 cups shredded Monterey Jack cheese (about 4 ounces)

Preheat oven to 400° F. Rub the butter over the inside surface of a 2-quart ovenproof casserole.

In a large bowl, whisk together the milk, eggs, melted butter, baking powder, baking soda, salt, and pepper. Stir in cornmeal and cream-style corn to make a batter. Spread half the batter in the buttered casserole. On top of this batter, spread half the chilies and half the cheese. Pour on remaining batter and top with remaining chilies and cheese. Bake 40 to 45 minutes, until bread is brown around the edges and set in the middle. It should still be moist and puddinglike in consistency. Cut into squares or wedges and serve warm.

Yield: 6–8 servings

In the South, spoon bread is often served in place of mashed potatoes.

◆ BASIC CORNMEAL MUFFINS ◆

1 cup milk
2 large eggs, lightly beaten
¼ cup vegetable oil
3 tablespoons sugar (optional)
1 tablespoon baking powder

1 teaspoon salt
1¼ cups cornmeal
*¾ cups all-purpose flour, preferably
  unbleached*

Preheat oven to 425° F. Line a 12-cup muffin tin with paper cups.

In a large mixing bowl whisk together the milk, eggs, and vegetable oil. Stir in sugar, baking powder, and salt. Stir in cornmeal and flour to make a batter. Fill muffin cups two-thirds full. Bake 15 to 20 minutes, until muffins turn golden brown. Remove muffin tin to wire rack. Cool 5 minutes before removing muffins from cups. Serve warm or cool completely and store in an airtight container at room temperature.

Yield: 12 muffins

Variation: For a sweeter, more cakelike muffin, add 2 tablespoons honey and 1 teaspoon vanilla.

• CORNMEAL MUFFINS WITH BACON •

1 cup yellow cornmeal
¾ cup all-purpose flour
3 teaspoons baking powder
5 teaspoons sugar
½ teaspoon salt
¼ teaspoon cayenne pepper
1 cup milk

1 cup corn kernels
2 eggs, lightly beaten
4 thick slices of bacon cooked to make a scant ½ cup crumbled bacon
2 tablespoons melted bacon fat or vegetable oil

Preheat oven to 400° F.

In a large bowl, mix together cornmeal, flour, baking powder, sugar, salt, and cayenne. In another bowl, combine milk, corn kernels, eggs, bacon, and bacon fat or vegetable oil. Mix well, then stir into dry ingredients to make a batter.

Pour into muffin tins (about ⅔ full) and bake about 25 to 30 minutes, until golden brown. Remove muffin tins to wire rack. Cool 5 minutes before removing muffins from cups. Serve warm or cool completely on racks and store in an airtight container at room temperature.

Yield: 12 muffins

Variation: If you are lucky enough to have a good country ham on hand, substitute ½ cup finely diced ham for the bacon.

◆ KATE'S CORN MUFFINS WITH STRAWBERRY JAM ◆

1 cup buttermilk or regular milk	1 tablespoon baking powder
2 large eggs	1/2 teaspoon salt
1/4 cup vegetable oil	1 cup yellow cornmeal
1 teaspoon vanilla extract	1 cup all-purpose flour
4 tablespoons sugar	1/3 cup strawberry jam, approximately

Preheat oven to 400° F. Line a 12-cup muffin tin with paper cups.

In a large mixing bowl, whisk together the buttermilk or milk, eggs, vegetable oil, and vanilla. Stir in sugar, baking powder, and salt. Stir in cornmeal and flour to make a batter. Spoon batter into muffin cups (about 2/3 full) then place a teaspoonful of jam in the center of each muffin. Bake for 20 to 25 minutes. Remove muffin tin to wire rack. Cool 5 minutes before removing muffins from cups. Serve warm or cool completely on racks and store in an airtight container at room temperature.

Yield: 12 muffins

• CORN PUFFS •

A good friend from Kentucky tells me that these puffs are called *zephyrs* back home, and that his are *always* made with white cornmeal.

½ cup cornmeal   1 cup boiling water
½ teaspoon salt   2 large eggs, separated
1 tablespoon butter

Preheat oven to 400° F. Grease a baking sheet.

   Place the cornmeal, salt, and butter in a heavy saucepan. Pour boiling water over cornmeal, stirring, and cook over low heat, stirring constantly, until mixture becomes thick. Remove from heat and allow to cool down enough to beat in the egg yolks without cooking them. Beat the egg whites until stiff and fold them into the mixture. Drop by teaspoonfuls onto the baking sheet. Bake about 20 minutes, until puffed up and delicately browned. Serve hot with lots of butter.

   Yield: about 20 puffs

• CORNMEAL CRISPS •

²⁄₃ cup yellow or white cornmeal
1 teaspoon salt
1 teaspoon sugar

2 tablespoons butter
¾ cup boiling water
¼ cup grated Cheddar cheese

Preheat oven to 425° F.

In a large mixing bowl combine cornmeal, salt, sugar, and butter. Pour boiling water over mixture and stir well to make a batter. Drop by teaspoonfuls onto buttered baking sheets, leaving plenty of room for batter to spread. Sprinkle with cheese. Bake about 10 minutes or until crackers turn golden brown. Remove from oven and let stand 10 to 15 minutes before moving crackers to a wire rack to cool.

Yield: 1 dozen crisps

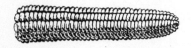

◆ LEMON CORN CAKE ◆

A simple but delicious cake that keeps well and is enjoyable at any time of day.

½ cup unsalted butter
¾ cup sugar
2 large eggs

Grated rind and juice of 1 lemon
¾ cup yellow cornmeal

Preheat oven to 350° F. Butter a 7-inch-round cake pan and line the bottom with parchment or waxed paper.

Cream together the butter and sugar. Beat in the eggs, lemon rind, and lemon juice. Stir in cornmeal. Pour cake batter into the cake pan and bake for about 40 minutes or until top is lightly browned and the sides have turned crisp. Remove from cake pan to cooling rack. Let cool before serving.

Yield: about 6 servings

◆ CORNMEAL SUGAR COOKIES ◆

¾ cup butter

1 cup brown sugar

1 large egg

1 teaspoon vanilla

1 cup flour

1 cup cornmeal

1 teaspoon salt

1½ teaspoons baking powder

Cream butter and sugar together. Beat egg lightly together with vanilla and beat into butter mixture. Mix flour, cornmeal, salt, and baking powder together and stir into the butter mixture. Divide the dough into three equal parts and roll into logs about 1 inch in diameter. Wrap each cookie log in plastic and chill in refrigerator for several hours or overnight. (Can stay in refrigerator for 1 week.)

Preheat oven to 400° F. Lightly grease cookie sheets.

Slice cookie logs into rounds approximately ¼ inch thick and bake on cookie sheets for 10 to 12 minutes, or until golden. Cool cookies on wire racks.

Yield: about 3 dozen cookies

Corn from the Griddle

Griddle Cakes,
Johnnycakes, Corn
Fritters, Hush Puppies,
Stuffings

• CORN PANCAKES •

½ cup all-purpose flour
¼ cup cornmeal
2 teaspoons baking powder
1 tablespoon sugar
Salt to taste
½ cup milk

2 tablespoons corn oil
1 egg, beaten
½ cup cooked fresh, canned, or frozen
   corn kernels (about 1 ear of corn)
Vegetable oil for griddle

In a large bowl, combine flour, cornmeal, baking powder, sugar, and salt. Whisk together milk, oil, and egg. Stir in corn. Stir milk mixture into flour mixture until just blended.

Lightly oil a griddle and heat until hot. Using ¼ to ⅓ cup batter per pancake, bake until golden, turn, and cook other side. Serve hot with maple syrup. Pancakes can be kept warm on a cookie sheet in a warm (250° F.) oven, but do not stack the warming pancakes.

Yield: 6 pancakes

◆ CORN AND BLUEBERRY PANCAKES ◆

I first had these yummy pancakes at my cousin's house in Maine. Their tiny wild blueberries are perfect for these pancakes because each berry is no larger than a corn kernel, but cultivated blueberries are delicious, too.

1½ cups corn kernels (about 3 ears of corn)
1 cup milk
2 eggs
3 tablespoons melted butter
1 teaspoon baking powder

¼ teaspoon salt
½ cup stone-ground yellow cornmeal
½ cup all-purpose flour
1 cup fresh blueberries, picked over and washed

Place the corn kernels in the bowl of a food processor or blender and whirl for a few seconds. Remove to a large mixing bowl and add the milk, eggs, and most of the melted butter, leaving a little to grease the griddle. Use a wire whisk to blend well. Stir in baking powder and salt, then add cornmeal and flour to make a batter. Stir in the blueberries.

Grease the griddle with remaining melted butter and heat it until it is very hot. Pour out ¼ cup of batter and cook pancakes about 3 minutes on one side and 2 minutes on the other. Continue cooking until all are done. Serve with maple or blueberry syrup. Pancakes can be kept warm on a cookie sheet in a warm (250° F.) oven, but do not stack the warming pancakes.

Yield: about 20 three-inch pancakes

• PUMPKIN CORN CAKES •

Corn and pumpkins form a perfect natural combination in these unusually good griddle cakes.

½ cup yellow cornmeal
1 cup boiling water
½ cup cooked pumpkin (canned is okay)
1 cup milk, scalded and cooled
1 large egg
1 cup all-purpose flour

2 teaspoons baking powder
2 teaspoons sugar
1 teaspoon allspice
¾ teaspoon salt
Vegetable oil for griddle

In a large mixing bowl, combine cornmeal and boiling water and let stand 5 minutes. Mash the pumpkin with a fork and add to cornmeal mixture. Add cooled milk and egg and stir until smooth. Sift together the flour, baking powder, sugar, allspice, and salt. Stir into cornmeal mixture to make a batter. Grease a griddle and heat until it is hot. Drop batter by tablespoonfuls and bake until bubbles form all over, turn, and bake other side until golden and crisp. Serve with maple syrup. Cakes can be kept warm on a cookie sheet in a warm (250° F.) oven, but do not stack the warming cakes.

Yield: 10–12 griddle cakes

• CORNMEAL RICE CAKES •

2 cups buttermilk
2 large eggs, separated
2 tablespoons vegetable oil
1 tablespoon sugar
1 teaspoon salt

½ teaspoon baking soda
1 cup cooked brown rice
½ cup stone-ground cornmeal
½ cup whole-wheat flour
Vegetable oil for griddle

In a large bowl, whisk together the buttermilk, eggs, and vegetable oil. Stir in the sugar, salt, and baking soda. Stir in the rice, cornmeal, and whole-wheat flour, just to blend. Brush griddle with vegetable oil and heat until very hot. Use a ¼-cup measuring cup to pour batter onto hot griddle. Cook about 3 minutes per side until done. Serve with your favorite syrup or preserves. Cakes can be kept warm on a cookie sheet in a warm (250° F.) oven, but do not stack the warming cakes.

Yield: 4–6 servings

• FRESH CORN CAKES •

Rich and delicate, these cakes make an elegant breakfast, brunch, or appetizer when served with smoked salmon and red caviar.

2 cups fresh corn kernels (about 4 ears of corn)
½ cup milk
½ cup butter, melted
1 large egg

1 cup all-purpose flour
Salt to taste
Freshly ground black pepper to taste
2 tablespoons butter

In the bowl of a food processor or blender, combine the corn kernels, milk, butter, and egg. Blend until kernels are pulverized and well blended. Add flour, salt, and pepper and blend well. Melt butter in a skillet and drop in batter by tablespoonfuls. Fry 2 to 3 minutes on each side, until golden brown.

Yield: 4 servings

My legs are stiff. I am cold. But the kitchen is warm. I can see the fire shining through the open hearth of the stove. The teakettle sings, the lid dances, a fine graceful flow of steam rises toward the ceiling and flattens at the top. Something smells good. Something warm, fragrant—johnnycake!

—*Della T. Lutes*, The Country Kitchen

• RHODE ISLAND JOHNNYCAKES •

These are nice fat johnnycakes—simple to make and simply delicious. Fresh, stone-ground cornmeal is a must. In the South these are called hoecakes and the sugar is left out.

1 cup white stone-ground cornmeal	*1 teaspoon sugar*
1 teaspoon salt	*1½ cups boiling water*

In a small bowl, mix together the cornmeal, salt, and sugar. Pour in the boiling water in a fine stream, stirring constantly. The batter will be very thick.

Drop by tablespoonfuls onto a hot, well-greased frying pan or griddle. Once you drop them, leave them alone for 5 minutes. Then turn over and cook for another 5 minutes. The finished johnnycakes should be about ½-inch thick. Cakes can be kept warm on a cookie sheet in a warm (250° F.) oven, but do not stack the warming cakes.

Yield: 8–10 johnnycakes

Some call them johnnycakes, some call them journey cakes, others insist that they are really Shawnee cakes, because they were first made by the Shawnee Indians to be used on journeys as they kept well for a long time.

◆ CRISPY CORN FRITTERS ◆

½ cup milk
2 large eggs
2 tablespoons melted butter
2 teaspoons baking powder
1 teaspoon salt

2½ cups fresh corn kernels (about 5 ears
of corn)
1¼ cups all-purpose flour
½ cup vegetable oil or clarified butter

In a large bowl, whisk together the milk, eggs, and melted butter. Stir in baking powder and salt. Stir in corn kernels and flour. Heat about 2 tablespoons of oil or clarified butter in a heavy skillet until very hot and drop fritter batter by tablespoonfuls into the skillet. Do not overcrowd the fritters. Fry until edges start to brown, turn over, and fry on other side. Fritters should be crispy and golden brown. Remove to a platter lined with paper towels to drain. Add 2 tablespoons of oil or batter for each batch of fritters. (Fritters may be kept warm in a 250° F. oven.) Serve with any ham or chicken dish or on their own with maple syrup.

Yield: 16–20 fritters

Note: These may also be deep-fried. Heat 3 to 4 cups vegetable oil to 375° F. and fry fritters 2 to 3 minutes, until golden brown.

◆ CORN-CLAM FRITTERS ◆

1 pint shucked clams with their juice
Milk, if needed
2 large eggs
2 tablespoons melted butter
2 teaspoons baking powder
1 teaspoon salt
2 cups fresh corn kernels (about 4 ears of
corn)

1 small onion, finely minced
½ teaspoon Worcestershire sauce
¼ teaspoon Tabasco sauce
Freshly ground black pepper to taste
1½ cups all-purpose flour
½ cup vegetable oil or clarified butter

Chop the clams, drain them, and save the liquid. Measure the liquid and milk to make ¾ cup total.

In a large bowl, whisk together the clam juice, eggs, and melted butter. Stir in baking powder and salt. Stir in chopped clams, corn kernels, minced onion, Worcestershire sauce, Tabasco sauce, and black pepper. Stir in the flour.

Heat about 2 tablespoons of oil or clarified butter in heavy skillet until very hot and drop fritter batter by tablespoonfuls into the skillet. Do not overcrowd the fritters. Fry until edges start to brown, turn over, and fry on other side. Fritters should be crispy and golden brown. Remove to a platter lined with paper towels to drain. Add 2 tablespoons of oil or butter for each batch of fritters. (Fritters may be kept warm in a 250° F. oven.)

Serve with tomato sauce or remoulade sauce.

Yield: 16–20 fritters

These are traditionally served with fried fish but I like to serve them with any seafood chowder.

3–4 cups vegetable or peanut oil, for
  frying
¾ cup buttermilk
1 large egg
1 large onion, finely chopped

2 teaspoons baking powder
1 teaspoon baking soda
1 teaspoon salt
1½ cups yellow cornmeal
½ cup all-purpose flour

Put enough oil in a deep, heavy kettle or deep-fat fryer to come halfway up the sides of the pot. Use a deep-fry thermometer to measure the temperature and heat oil to 360° F.

In a large bowl, whisk together the buttermilk, egg, and onion. Stir in baking powder, baking soda, and salt. Stir in cornmeal and flour to make a dough stiff enough to hold its shape. Use 2 soup spoons to shape dough into balls about the size of an egg. Drop into hot fat and fry until golden brown, about 3 to 4 minutes. Turn over once after about 2 minutes. Remove hush puppies with a long-handled slotted spoon and drain on paper towels. Continue frying until all are done but bring the oil up to 360° F. between batches.

Yield: 12 hush puppies

Variations:

1. Add any herbs you like to the batter.

2. If you prefer you can fry these in a skillet in butter or a combination of oil and butter.

• CORN BREAD STUFFING •

1 pound pork sausage meat
4 tablespoons butter
3 large celery stalks, diced
1 large onion, diced
4 cloves garlic, minced
1 corn bread made day before*

1/2 cup finely chopped parsley
1/2 cup finely chopped scallions
1/2 teaspoon dried thyme
1 teaspoon freshly ground black pepper
1 1/2 cups (approximately) chicken or
   turkey stock

In a large sauté pan, cook the sausage meat, stirring frequently with a wooden spoon to break up the lumps, until well browned (about 20 minutes). Turn off heat and remove sausage meat with a slotted spoon and reserve.

Add butter to the drippings and sauté celery, onion, and garlic until just softened. Do not brown. Remove from heat, crumble the corn bread and add it to the vegetables. Add the reserved sausage meat, parsley, scallions, thyme, and pepper. Toss all ingredients until lightly blended. Add just enough stock to moisten the stuffing to the consistency you like.

This makes enough stuffing for one 12- to 14-pound turkey, or two 6-pound chickens. Or, spoon the stuffing into a well-greased 9 × 13-inch baking dish, cover with foil, and bake in a low (325° F.) oven for 1 hour. Uncover and bake 15 more minutes if you like a crispy top.

*Choose from among Southern Corn Bread, page 92; Buttermilk Corn Bread, page 89; Blue-Corn Skillet Bread, page 91; or Summer Corn Bread, page 93.

This is an old-time version of stovetop stuffing and an economical and delicious way to use up leftover corn bread. Serve it with any meat or chicken instead of rice or potatoes.

4 tablespoons butter or margarine
1 medium onion, chopped fine
2 stalks celery, chopped fine
4 cups of cooked corn bread, broken by
    hand into small pieces

¼ teaspoon dried thyme
¼ teaspoon dried sage
Salt to taste
Freshly ground black pepper to taste
½ to 1 cup water or chicken broth

Melt the butter or margarine in a large heavy skillet. Sauté the onion and celery until softened, about 10 minutes. In a bowl, mix the corn bread, thyme, sage, salt, pepper, and just enough water or chicken broth to make the mixture the consistency of stuffing. Add the corn bread mixture to the skillet with the onions and celery and fry gently over medium heat until golden brown and crusty on the bottom.

Yield: 6 servings

Variation: Add some crumbled bacon pieces to the corn bread mixture and fry in bacon fat or part bacon fat, part butter.

Corn in the Pantry

Relishes and Preserves

Corn Is More Than Food

. . . *one part or another of the versatile crop has been implanted in—along with such routine products as corn syrup, corn oil, cornmeal, and corncob pipes—automobile paint, potato chips, plastics, ice cream, tires, leather, chewing gum, textiles, library paste, clam chowder, dog biscuits, spaghetti sauce, table mats, salad dressing, sausages, foot powder, gunpowder, face powder, table salt, mince meat, mustard, mayonnaise, ketchup, peanut butter, dice, licorice, oilcloth, sandpaper, soap, drinking straws, surgical dressings, insecticides, boot polish, children's dolls, lactic acid, jelly candy, artificial silk, embalming fluid, scratchless polishers for jewelry and ball bearings, nail-polish remover, hair tonic, rubbing alcohol, ether, deodorants, mattresses, varnish, hydraulic-brake fluid, gasohol, adhesive tape, fireworks, film, safety glass, and—of all things—agricultural poisons.*

—E. J. Kahn, Jr., The Staffs of Life

• CORN CABBAGE RELISH •

4 cups fresh corn kernels (about 8 ears of corn)
4 cups coarsely chopped onions
4 cups peeled and chopped ripe tomatoes
4 cups peeled, seeded, and chopped cucumbers
3 cups coarsely chopped cabbage
2 green bell peppers, chopped

2 red bell peppers, chopped
3 cups white vinegar
1 cup water
2 cups sugar
2 tablespoons kosher salt
1½ teaspoons dry mustard
1 tablespoon celery seeds
1 tablespoon pickling spice

Sterilize 6 1-pint canning jars and lids according to manufacturer's directions.

Combine all the ingredients in a large pot. Bring slowly to a boil, reduce heat, and simmer for 30 minutes, stirring frequently. Pour into hot, sterilized jars, leaving ½-inch headroom, and seal with sterilized lids according to manufacturer's instructions. Place jars on a rack in a large pot and add boiling water to cover tops of jars by at least 2 inches. Keep water at a boil for 15 to 20 minutes. Remove jars to a towel-covered surface to cool.

Yield: 6 pints

Note: If you are going to consume the relish within a week's time you can skip the steps to sterilize the jars and the final hot water bath.

• CORN PRESERVES •

Sweet, spicy-hot, and delicious. Try a toasted bagel with cream cheese topped with corn preserves for a new breakfast treat. You can put these preserves in canning jars and save them for the winter or refrigerate and use within two weeks.

2 quarts water
1 teaspoon salt
3 cups fresh corn kernels (about 6 ears of corn)
1 red bell pepper, stemmed, seeded, and finely diced

3 fresh jalapeño peppers, finely diced
½ teaspoon cayenne
5 cups sugar
1½ cups white vinegar
6 ounces liquid fruit pectin

Sterilize 2 1-pint jars or 4 half-pint canning jars and lids according to manufacturer's directions.

Bring water and salt to a boil and add corn kernels, red bell pepper, jalapeño peppers, and cayenne. Cook 5 minutes, drain, and reserve.

Bring sugar and vinegar to a boil, stirring until sugar melts. Add pectin and when liquid returns to a boil, remove from heat. Stir in corn and peppers. Pour into hot, sterilized jars, leaving ½-inch headroom, and seal with sterilized lids according to manufacturer's instructions. Place jars on a rack in a large pot and add boiling water to cover tops of jars by at least 2 inches. Keep water at a boil for 15 to 20 minutes. Remove jars to a towel-covered surface to cool.

Yield: 2 pints

⋄ CORNCOB JELLY ⋄

This is also called Poor Man's Jelly, and although it may seem like a lot of trouble to go to for a little corn flavor, you may turn out to be like me, and find this delicate corn-flavored jelly totally addictive.

12 corncobs
6 cups water, or enough to cover the corncobs

1 package (1¾ ounces) powdered fruit pectin
3 cups sugar

Sterilize 4 ½-pint canning jars and lids according to manufacturer's directions.

Use a cleaver to chop up the cobs into thirds or fourths and place them in a large pot. Add the water and bring to a boil. Simmer for 40 minutes or until liquid has reduced by almost half. Measure three cups of the juice from this and place in a smaller saucepan. Add powdered pectin and bring to a boil. Add the sugar and boil for 1 minute. Remove from heat, skim, and pour into hot, sterilized jars, leaving ½-inch headroom, and seal with sterilized lids according to manufacturer's instructions.

Yield: 4 half-pints

Colorful ornamental corn with kernels in vivid shades of orange, red, maroon, and purple is not edible. This Indian or squaw corn is found at farmstands in the autumn months and makes a charming decoration for the house and table.

Corncobs are sweet. Their smoke is deliciously sweet for curing hams and bacon. These days they are being ground up and included in cattle feed. In pioneer Nebraska cobs were boiled down to a sweet syrup that was harder to obtain but finer flavored than sorghum molasses. A similar product was corncob jelly, one of the prettiest-colored and delicately flavored jellies imaginable.

—*Roger L. and Linda K. Welsch*, Cather's Kitchens

Corn at the Movies

Today, millions of Americans who sit munching popcorn before flickering movie screens, television sets, and fireplaces are following an ancient tradition. Throughout much of the hemisphere generations of Indians popped corn in earthen vessels and ate it around open fires. One-thousand-year-old specimens of the grain from ancient, musty Peruvian tombs still popped when heated!

—*Nicholas P. Hardeman,* Shucks, Shocks, and Hominy Blocks— Corn as a Way of Life in Pioneer America

Popcorn was a distinct variety of corn, like dent corn or flour corn. It was cultivated by the Incas and used to decorate bodies for burial. Today it is the mainstay of the U.S. film industry. Without the profits of their concession stands, probably half the movie theaters in America would close down. Popcorn makers used to expand a kernel of popcorn fifteen times its original size; now they puff a kernel to forty times its size and even more so, so a quart-size cup of popcorn, chewed with eyes glued to the Technicolor Cinerama screen, contains only about an ounce of corn.

—*James Trager,* The Food Book

• POPCORN •

Popcorn is the all-American snack and has been popular since the Indians brought some to the first Thanksgiving. Today, there seems to be a great revival of home-made popcorn, perhaps to go with all the video movies people are watching, perhaps because all those dieters have discovered that 1 cup of popcorn without any butter has a mere 25 calories.

Today there are special electric popcorn poppers for the home, and popcorn kernels to pop in the microwave. But all popcorn is easy to make and, even without special equipment, anyone can make perfectly delicious perfectly popped corn at home in just a few minutes. Use either a heavy skillet with a lid or a large pot with a lid. I use the same pot I cook spaghetti in. If you are using an electric popper or microwave popcorn, follow the manufacturer's directions.

2 tablespoons vegetable oil   *½ cup popcorn kernels*

Put the oil in a skillet or large pot and place on high heat. Wait 1 minute and drop in one or two kernels of corn. When the kernels pop, add the rest of the corn kernels. Cover the skillet or pot and shake the pan to move the corn kernels around. The lid should fit loosely enough for the steam to escape as the corn pops. Continue cooking and shaking until the popping sounds slow down, about 2 or 3 minutes. Remove from heat and pour popcorn into a large serving bowl.

Yield: 6–8 cups popped corn

Serve with one of the following toppings.

• MELTED BUTTER AND SALT •

3 to 4 tablespoons butter   ½ teaspoon salt

Melt the butter in a small saucepan and drizzle over popcorn. Sprinkle with salt and toss to mix well.

• GARLIC BUTTER •

3 to 4 tablespoons butter   ½ teaspoon salt
1 to 2 cloves garlic, crushed

Melt the butter in a small saucepan, add the crushed garlic, and cook for 1 minute over low heat. Do not burn the butter or the garlic. Drizzle garlic butter over popcorn, sprinkle with salt, and toss to mix.

Variation: Add 1 to 2 tablespoons finely chopped parsley at the very end.

◆ PESTO BUTTER ◆

1 to 2 tablespoons butter
2 tablespoons olive oil
2 cloves garlic, crushed

½ cup freshly grated Parmesan cheese
2 tablespoons finely shredded fresh basil

Heat the butter and olive oil in a small saucepan until butter is melted. Add the crushed garlic and cook for 1 minute over low heat. Do not burn the butter or the garlic. Remove from heat, stir in Parmesan cheese and basil. Drizzle over popcorn and toss to mix.

Variation: If you want to get really fancy, toast ½ cup of pine nuts in a skillet until just golden and toss with popcorn at the end.

◆ CHILI BUTTER ◆

3 to 4 tablespoons butter
3 scallions, finely sliced
1 teaspoon hot chili powder

½ teaspoon cumin
½ teaspoon salt

Melt the butter in a small saucepan, add the scallions, chili powder, cumin, and salt. Drizzle over popcorn and toss to mix.

Variation: Add 1 teaspoon finely chopped fresh coriander.

• FRESH HERB POPCORN •

Choose from whatever fresh herbs are available to you, in any combination.

3 to 4 tablespoons butter
½ teaspoon salt
1 tablespoon finely chopped parsley
1 tablespoon finely chopped dill

1 tablespoon finely chopped basil
1 tablespoon finely chopped rosemary
1 tablespoon thyme leaves
1 tablespoon finely chopped chives

Melt the butter in a small saucepan and drizzle over popcorn. Sprinkle with salt and toss to mix well. Add the fresh herbs and toss again.

Why does popcorn pop? Popcorn kernels are made up of a layer of very hard starch wrapped around a soft core that contains moisture. When the corn kernel is heated, the moisture inside turns to steam, building up pressure until the kernel explodes. The hard kernels in the bottom of the pot that never popped had probably dried out and lost their little moist core.

◆ CHEESY POPCORN ◆

3 to 4 tablespoons butter   *½ cup grated sharp cheddar cheese*

Melt the butter and drizzle over popcorn. Sprinkle with cheese and toss to mix well.

Variation: Instead of cheddar use ½ cup crumbled feta cheese or crumbled blue cheese or try ½ cup of crumbled goat cheese.

It was once a custom at rural American husking bees that whoever found a colored ear could kiss the person of his or her choice. The custom may have originated with the Iroquois Indians, who had a similar, though lustier custom.

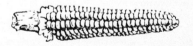

INDEX